Experiencing
Choral Music

ADVANCED

SO-BYN-376

SIGHT-SINGING

Developed by

HAL•LEONARD®
CORPORATION

Mc Graw Hill **Glencoe**

New York, New York   Columbus, Ohio   Chicago, Illinois   Peoria, Illinois   Woodland Hills, California

The portions of the National Standards for Music Education included here are reprinted from *National Standards for Arts Education* with permission from MENC–The National Association for Music Education. All rights reserved. Copyright © 1994 by MENC. The complete National Standards and additional materials relating to the Standards are available from MENC, 1806 Robert Fulton Drive, Reston, VA 20191 (telephone 800-336-3768).

A portion of the sales of this material goes to support music education programs through programs of MENC–The National Association for Music Education.

Glencoe

The *McGraw·Hill* Companies

Printed in the United States of America.

Send all inquiries to:
Glencoe/McGraw-Hill
21600 Oxnard Street, Suite 500
Woodland Hills, CA 91367

ISBN 0-07-861132-6

2 3 4 5 6 7 8 9   045   09 08 07 06 05

Credits

AUTHORS

Emily Crocker
Vice President of Choral Publications
Hal Leonard Corporation, Milwaukee, Wisconsin
Founder and Artistic Director, Milwaukee Children's Choir

Audrey Snyder
Composer
Eugene, Oregon

EDITORIAL

Linda Rann
Senior Editor
Hal Leonard Corporation, Milwaukee, Wisconsin

Stacey Nordmeyer
Choral Editor
Hal Leonard Corporation, Milwaukee, Wisconsin

Table of Contents

CHAPTER 4

CHAPTER 5

CHAPTER 6

CHAPTER 7

CHAPTER 8

CHAPTER 9

CHAPTER 10

TO THE STUDENT

Welcome to choir!

By singing in the choir, you have chosen to be a part of an exciting and rewarding adventure. The benefits of being in choir are many. Basically, singing is fun. It provides an expressive way of sharing your feelings and emotions. Through choir, you will have friends that share a common interest with you. You will experience the joy of making beautiful music together. Choir provides an opportunity to develop interpersonal skills. It takes teamwork and cooperation to sing together, and you must learn how to work with others. As you critique your individual and group performances, you can improve your ability to analyze and communicate your thoughts clearly.

Even if you do not pursue a music career, music can be an important part of your life. There are many avocational opportunities in music. **Avocational** means *not related to a job or career.* Singing as a hobby can provide you with personal enjoyment, enrich your life, and teach you life skills. Singing is something you can do for the rest of your life.

In this course, you will be presented with the basic skills of music notation and sight-singing. You will learn new concepts through exercises, combinable lines, speech choruses and original sight-singing practice songs. Guidelines for becoming a successful choir member include:

- Come to class prepared to learn.
- Respect the efforts of others.
- Work daily to improve your sight-singing skills.
- Sing expressively at all times.
- Have fun singing.

This book was written to provide you with a meaningful choral experience. Take advantage of the knowledge and opportunities offered here. Your exciting adventure of experiencing choral music is about to begin!

CHAPTER 1

Pitch

◆ The Circle of Fifths

In music, the relationship between each key is based on a perfect fifth. A **perfect fifth** is *an interval of two pitches that are five notes apart on the staff.* An easy way to visualize this relationship is on the keyboard.

Study the keyboard below. Notice that if you start on C and move to the left by the distance of a fifth, you will find the keys that contain flats. Notice that the number of flats in each key signature increases by one each time you move one perfect fifth to the left.

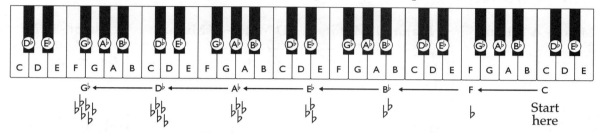

However, if you start on C and move to the right by the distance of a fifth, you will find the keys that contain sharps. Notice that the number of sharps in each key signature increases by one each time you move one perfect fifth to the right.

The Circle of Fifths is another easy way to visualize and memorize patterns of sharps, flats and key signatures.

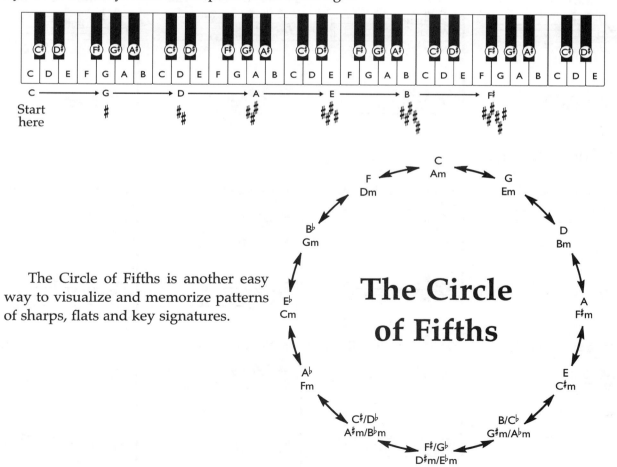

Pitch

◆ Key Signature

At the beginning of the staff, directly to the right of the clef is the key signature. The key signature identifies the keynote of the music. The sharps or flats in the key signature indicate all the pitches in the music that will be affected by the sharp or flat in the key signature.

◆ The Sharp Keys

◆ The Flat Keys

Pitch

◆ Scale and Key

A **scale** is *a group of notes that are sung or played in succession and are based on a particular home tone, or keynote.* A **half step** is *the smallest interval between two notes on a keyboard.* A **whole step** is *the combination of two half steps side by side.*

The major scale is a particular arrangement of whole steps and half steps:

$$W + W + H + W + W + W + H$$

Each major scale has a corresponding relative minor scale that shares the same key signature. The relative minor is the sixth degree of the major scale. Thus, C major (which has no sharps or flats) has A minor as its relative minor.

The minor scale is a particular arrangement of whole steps and half steps:

$$W + H + W + W + H + W + W$$

The sixth and seventh degrees of the minor scale are often raised.

◆ Primary Diatonic Chords

The **tonic chord** (**I** or "one" chord) is *a chord built on the keynote of a particular scale.* The primary diatonic chords of a particular key are the tonic (**I** or **i**), subdominant (**IV** or **iv**) and dominant (**V** or **v**) chords.

◆ Practice

Practice the scale, tonic chord and primary diatonic chords of the following major and minor scales. Use this scale skill bank as a resource in reading and sight-singing music.

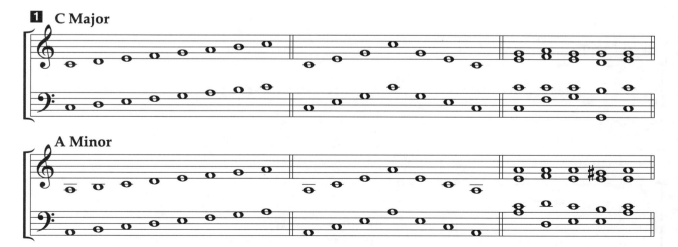

1 C Major

A Minor

2 G Major

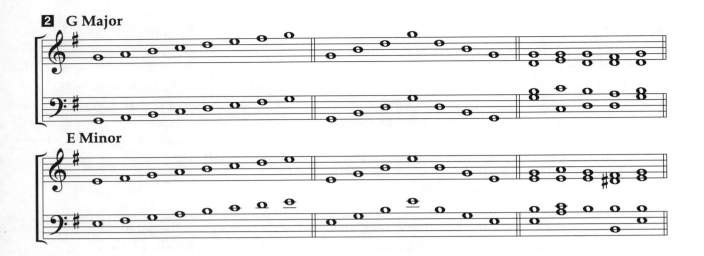

E Minor

3 D Major

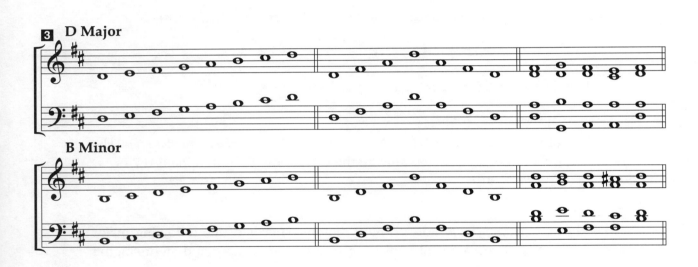

B Minor

4 A Major

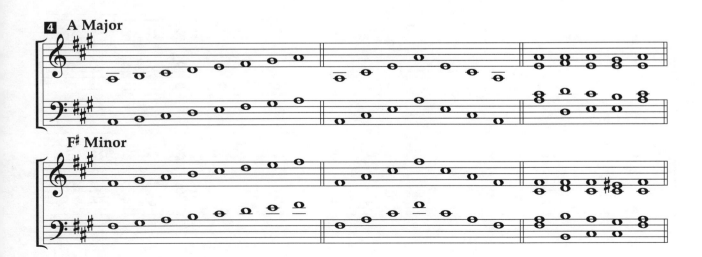

F# Minor

5 E Major

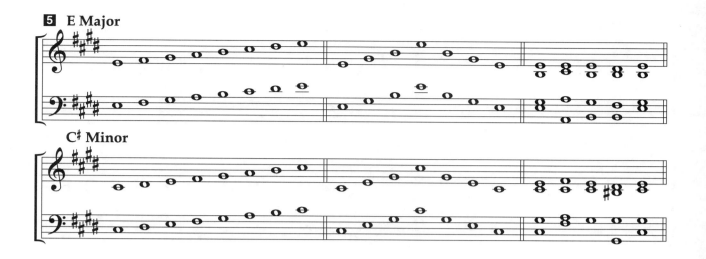

C# Minor

6 B Major

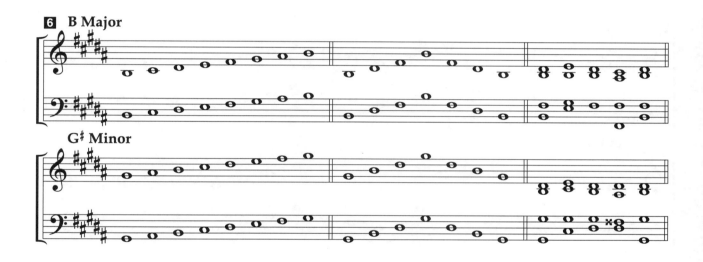

G# Minor

7 F# Major

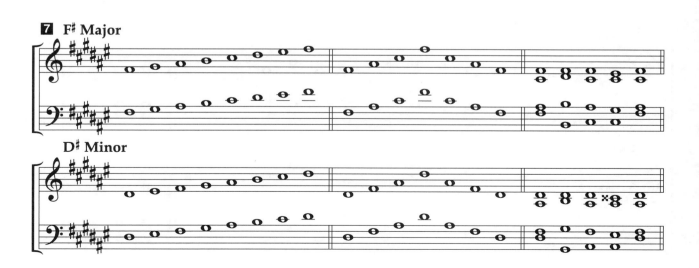

D# Minor

8 C♯ Major

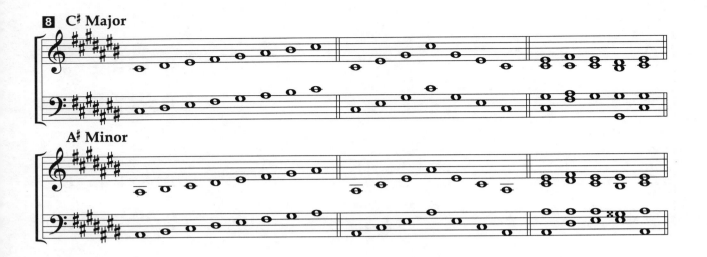

A♯ Minor

9 F Major

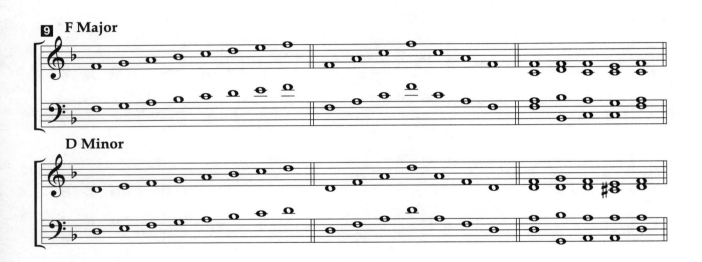

D Minor

10 B♭ Major

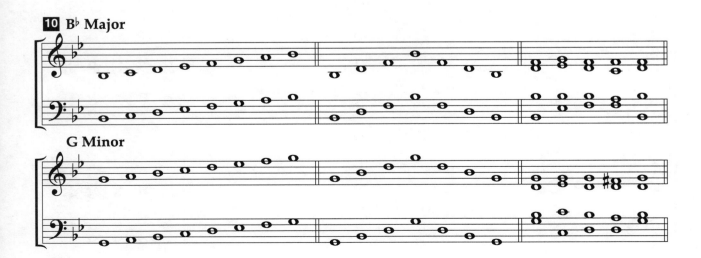

G Minor

11 E♭ Major

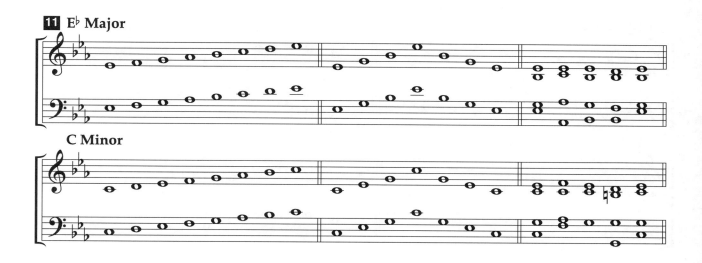

C Minor

12 A♭ Major

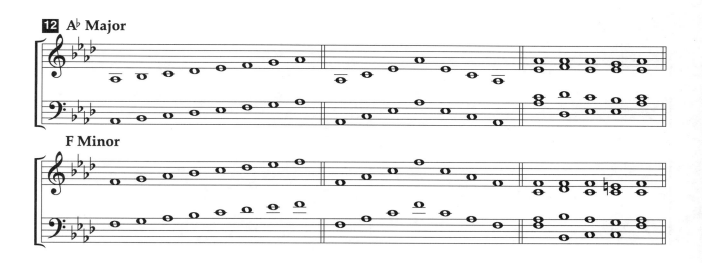

F Minor

13 D♭ Major

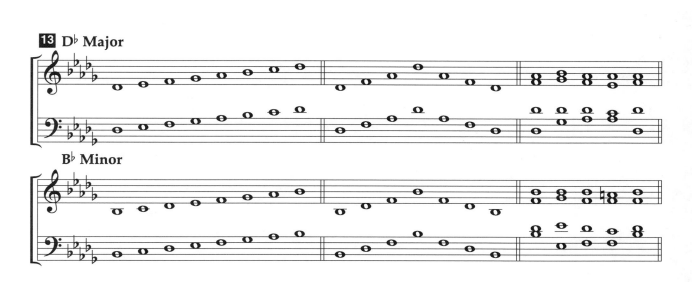

B♭ Minor

14 G♭ Major

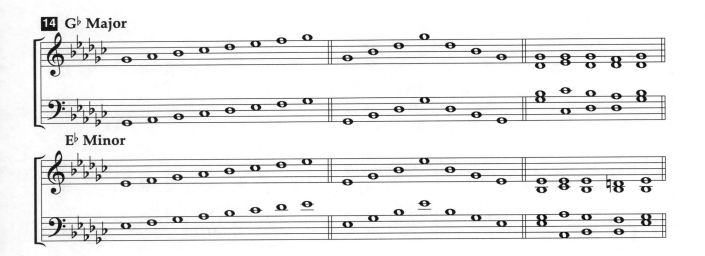

E♭ Minor

15 C♭ Major

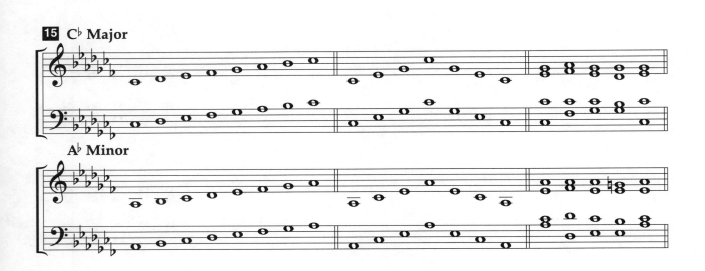

A♭ Minor

Pitch

◆ Diatonic and Chromatic Scales

A **diatonic scale** is *a scale that uses no altered pitches or accidentals.* Major and minor scales are examples of diatonic scales.

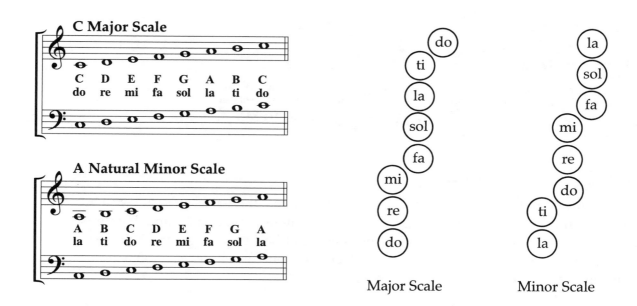

Major Scale   Minor Scale

The **chromatic scale** is *a scale that consists entirely of half steps and includes all 12 pitches within an octave.*

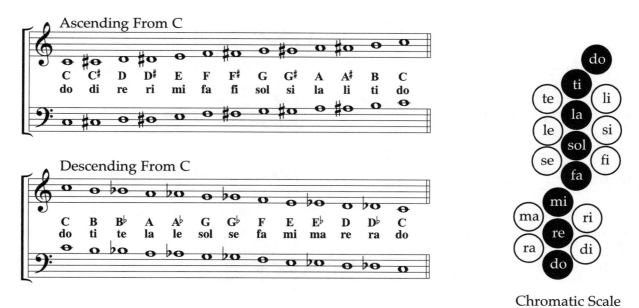

Chromatic Scale

Pitch

◆ Major and Minor Scales

Major and minor are two types of scales in music. The C major and C minor scales both start and end on C, but each have a different harmonic sound based on the arrangements of whole steps and half steps in the scales.

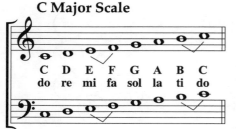

C Major Scale

C D E F G A B C
do re mi fa sol la ti do

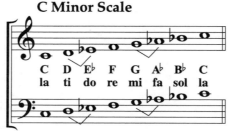

C Minor Scale

C D E♭ F G A♭ B♭ C
la ti do re mi fa sol la

∨ = half step

◆ Modes and Modal Scales

Before major and minor keys and scales were developed, there was an earlier system of pitch organization called modes. Like major and minor scales, each modal scale is made up of a specific arrangement of whole steps and half steps, with the half steps occurring between *mi* and *fa,* and *ti* and *do.* Here are some examples of modal scales starting and ending on C.

Like the major scale, the **Ionian scale** is *a scale that starts and ends on* do.

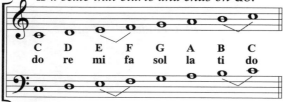

C D E F G A B C
do re mi fa sol la ti do

The **Dorian scale** is *a scale that starts and ends on* re.

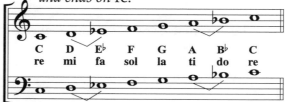

C D E♭ F G A B♭ C
re mi fa sol la ti do re

The **Phrygian scale** is *a scale that starts and ends on* mi.

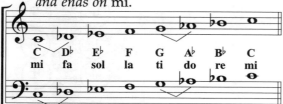

C D♭ E♭ F G A♭ B♭ C
mi fa sol la ti do re mi

The **Lydian scale** is *a scale that starts and ends on* fa.

C D E F♯ G A B C
fa sol la ti do re mi fa

The **Mixolydian scale** is *a scale that starts and ends on* sol.

C D E F G A B♭ C
sol la ti do re mi fa sol

Like the minor scale, the **Aeolian scale** is *a scale that starts and ends on* la.

C D E♭ F G A♭ B♭ C
la ti do re mi fa sol la

Evaluation

Demonstrate what you have learned in Chapter One by completing the following:

◆ **The Circle of Fifths**
Copy the following diagram on a separate sheet of paper and fill in the blanks with the correct key names.

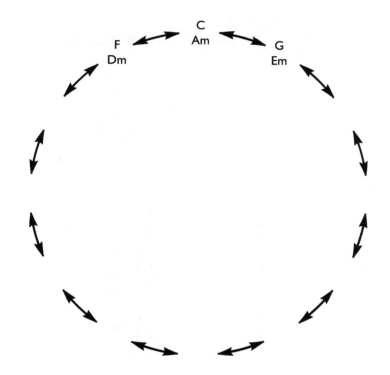

◆ Sight-sing the following melody. On which mode is it based?

Personent Hodie

Swedish Melody

re

CHAPTER 2

Rhythm

◆ The Beat

The **beat** is *the steady pulse of all music.* Music notes represent sound and music rests represent silence. **Rhythm** is *the combination of long and short notes and rests.* These notes and rests may move with the beat, faster than the beat or slower than the beat.

◆ Note and Rest Value Relationships

The following charts show basic notes and rests in their relationship to the beat and to each other.

Basic Note and Rest Values

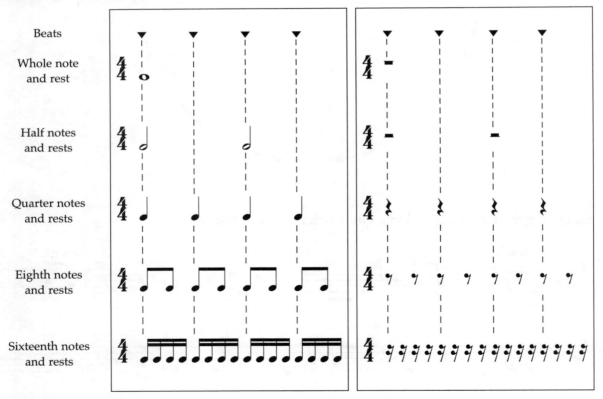

Rhythm

◆ ## Common Note and Rest Combinations

Dotted Note and Rest Combinations

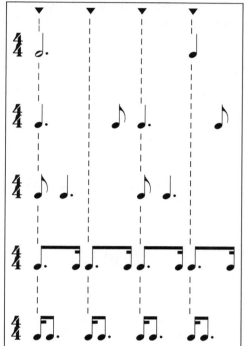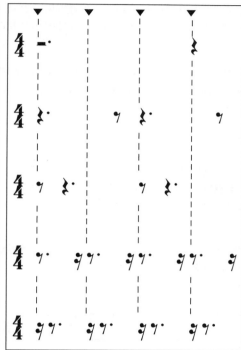

Other Note and Rest Combinations

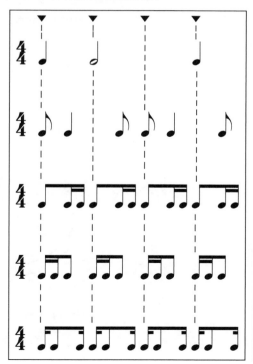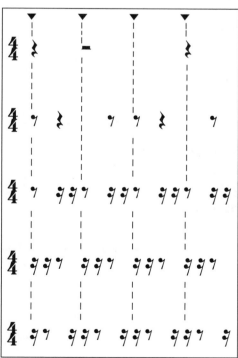

Rhythm

◆ Time Signature

Meter is a way of organizing rhythm. A **time signature** (sometimes called a meter signature) is *the set of numbers at the beginning of a piece of music which indicate the number of beats per measure, and the kind of note that receives the beat.* For example:

3 = The top number of the time signature indicates the number of beats per measure.
4 = The bottom number of the time signature indicates the kind of note that receives the beat.

◆ Simple Meter

Simple meter is *any meter in which the beat is divisible by two.* Following are the most common simple meters. Read and conduct each pattern.

2 = two beats per measure
4 = the quarter note receives the beat

Common rhythm patterns in $\frac{2}{4}$ meter:

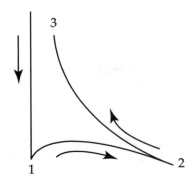

Conducting pattern

3 = three beats per measure
4 = the quarter note receives the beat

Common rhythm patterns in $\frac{3}{4}$ meter:

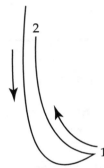

Conducting pattern

4 = four beats per measure
4 = the quarter note receives the beat

Common rhythm patterns in $\frac{4}{4}$ meter:

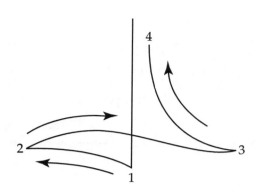

Conducting pattern

2 = two beats per measure
2 = the half note receives the beat

Common rhythm patterns in $\frac{2}{2}$ meter:

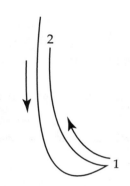

Conducting pattern

3 = three beats per measure
2 = the half note receives the beat

Common rhythm patterns in $\frac{3}{2}$ meter:

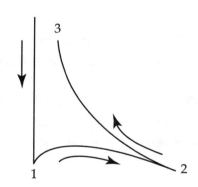

Conducting pattern

4 = four beats per measure
2 = the half note receives the beat

Common rhythm patterns in $\frac{4}{2}$ meter:

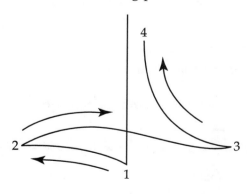

Conducting pattern

2 = two beats per measure
8 = the eighth note receives the beat

Common rhythm patterns in $\frac{2}{8}$ meter:

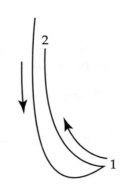

Conducting pattern

3 = three beats per measure
8 = the eighth note receives the beat

Common rhythm patterns in $\frac{3}{8}$ meter:

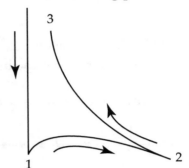

Conducting pattern

4 = four beats per measure
8 = the eighth note receives the beat

Common rhythm patterns in $\frac{4}{8}$ meter:

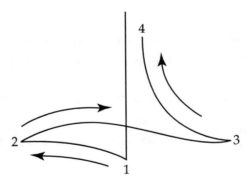

Conducting pattern

6 = six beats per measure
8 = the eighth note receives the beat

Common rhythm patterns in $\frac{6}{8}$ meter:

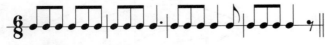

Slow tempo only (see compound meter for moderate tempo).

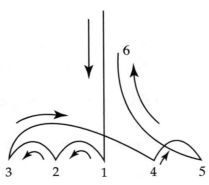

Conducting pattern

Rhythm

◆ Compound Meter

Compound meter is *any meter in which the beat is divided into multiples of three.* For example, $\frac{6}{8}$ meter is a compound meter since the beat is divided into two groups of three eighth notes each with two beats in a measure.

As in simple meters, compound meters are usually conducted in two, three or four, except when the tempo is very slow.

Following are the most common compound meters. Read and conduct each pattern.

6 = two beats per measure (the beats are made up of two groups of three eighth notes)

8 = the dotted quarter note receives the beat (except in a very slow tempo)

Common rhythm patterns in $\frac{6}{8}$ meter:

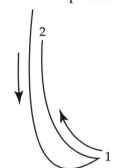

Conducting pattern

9 = three beats per measure (the beats are made up of three groups of three eighth notes)

8 = the dotted quarter note receives the beat (except in a very slow tempo)

Common rhythm patterns in $\frac{9}{8}$ meter:

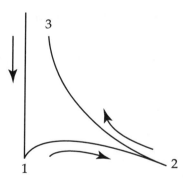

Conducting pattern

12 = four beats per measure (the beats are made up of four groups of three eighth notes)

8 = the dotted quarter note receives the beat (except in a very slow tempo)

Common rhythm patterns in $\frac{12}{8}$ meter:

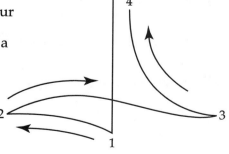

Conducting pattern

6 = two beats per measure (the beats are made up of two
groups of three quarter notes)
4 = the dotted half note receives the beat (except in a
very slow tempo)

Common rhythm patterns in **6/4** meter:

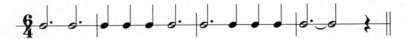

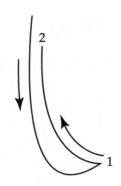

Conducting pattern

9 = three beats per measure (the beats are made up of
three groups of three quarter notes)
4 = the dotted half note receives the beat (except in a
very slow tempo)

Common rhythm patterns in **9/4** meter:

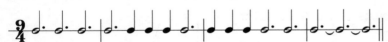

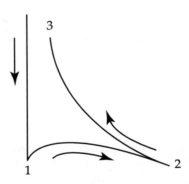

Conducting pattern

12 = four beats per measure (the beats are made up of
four groups of three quarter notes)
4 = the dotted half note receives the beat (except in a
very slow tempo)

Common rhythm patterns in **12/4** meter:

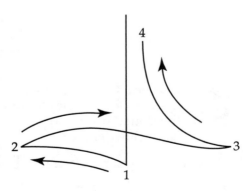

Conducting pattern

Rhythm

◆ Asymmetrical Meters

A common practice, especially in contemporary music, is the unequal grouping of beats.

◆ $\frac{5}{4}$ and $\frac{5}{8}$ Meter

$\frac{5}{4}$ and $\frac{5}{8}$ meters may be grouped as 2 + 3, or 3 + 2, and the beat patterns reflect these unequal groupings.

At a slow tempo:

3 + 2   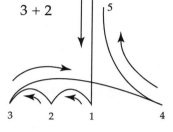   or   2 + 3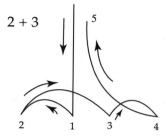

At a faster tempo, these meters are usually conducted in two.

3 + 2      2 + 3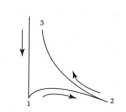

◆ $\frac{7}{4}$ and $\frac{7}{8}$ Meter

$\frac{7}{4}$ and $\frac{7}{8}$ meters may be grouped as 3 + 2 + 2, or 2 + 2 + 3, and the beat patterns reflect these unequal groupings.

$\frac{7}{4}$ and $\frac{7}{8}$ meters are usually conducted in three.

3 + 2 + 2   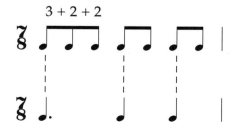   2 + 2 + 3

Rhythm

◆ Borrowed Division • Triplets

Sometimes in simple meter, there is a need for the beat to be divided into three. This is called borrowed division of the beat, and is indicated by a triplet. A triplet is notated with a small 3 centered above or below the group of notes. Sometimes a bracket is also used.

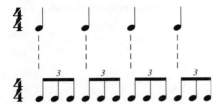

Following are common rhythmic patterns using triplets. Read each pattern.

Any note value can be a triplet. In simple meter, a quarter note triplet occupies the same amount of time as two quarter notes or one half note. A half note triplet occupies the same amount of time as two half notes or one whole note.

Quarter Note Triplets   Half Note Triplets

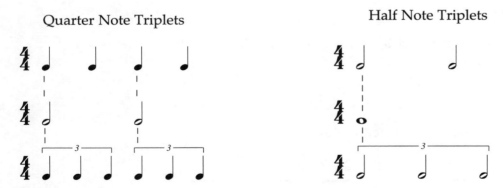

Following are common rhythm patterns using quarter note and half note triplets. Read the patterns.

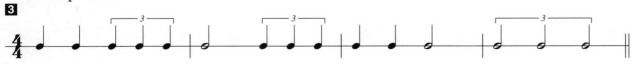

Rhythm

◆ Borrowed Division • Duplets

Sometimes in compound meter, there is a need for the beat to be divided into two. This is called borrowed division of the beat, and is indicated by a duplet. Sometimes a bracket is also used.

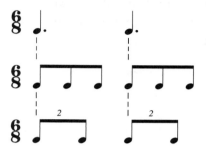

Following are common rhythmic patterns using duplets. Read each pattern.

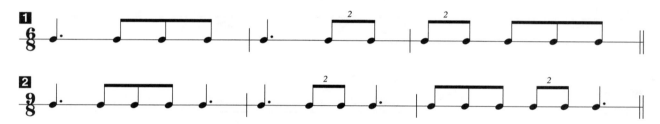

Any note value can be a duplet. In compound meter, a quarter note duplet occupies the same amount of time as three quarter notes or one dotted half note.

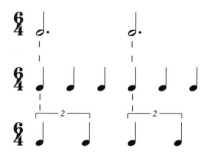

Following are common rhythm patterns using quarter note duplets. Read each pattern.

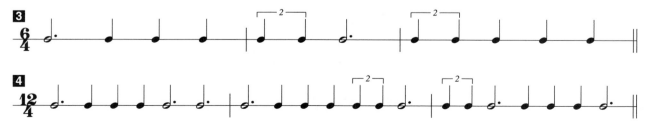

Evaluation

Demonstrate what you have learned in Chapter Two by completing the following:

◆ Be A Composer

For each of the time signatures listed below, copy the measures on a separate sheet of paper and write a four-measure rhythm pattern that uses a variety of notes and rests in correct combinations. Be sure to include triplet and duplet examples in some of your rhythm patterns. Clap or play the patterns on rhythm instruments.

1
$\frac{2}{2}$

2
$\frac{3}{8}$

3
$\frac{6}{4}$

4
$\frac{5}{8}$

5
$\frac{7}{4}$

6
$\frac{9}{8}$

Pitch

◆ Diatonic Intervals

An **interval** is *the relationship of one note to another.* **Diatonic intervals** are *the relationships of the notes that naturally occur within the scale of the key* (do, re, mi, fa, sol, la and ti).

The interval from one note to another is given a number, depending upon the distance between the two notes. For example, the distance from *do* to *mi* is called a "third" (3rd) because *do* and *mi* are three notes apart (*do, re* and *mi*). Sing the following diatonic intervals in the key of C major.

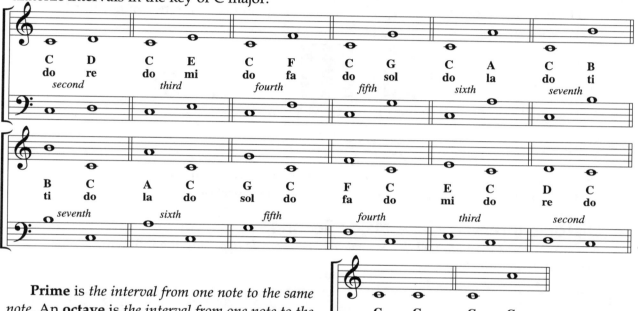

Prime is *the interval from one note to the same note.* An **octave** is *the interval from one note to the same note that is eight notes apart.*

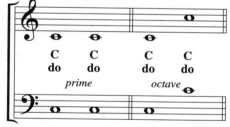

◆ Practice

Identify the intervals in the following examples, then read and echo each interval. Sing in the octave that best fits your range.

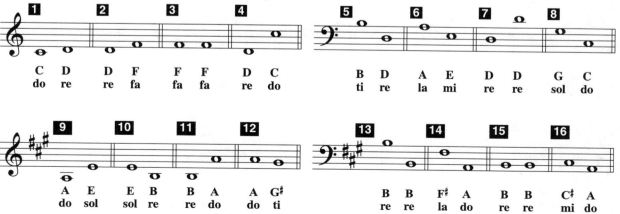

Pitch

◆ Major and Minor Diatonic Intervals

Each diatonic interval may be further classified by its number of whole steps and half steps. For example, the interval of a third may be called a "major third" or a "minor third."

A **major third** is *an interval that is made up of two whole steps side by side.* A **minor third** is *an interval that is made up of one whole step and one half step side by side.* Using the keyboard below, notice that in the key of C major, the interval from *do* to *mi* (C to E) is made up of two whole steps and is therefore a major third. Note that the interval from *mi* to *sol* (E to G) is made up of one whole step plus one half step and is therefore a minor third.

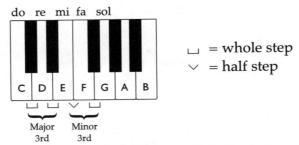

⊔ = whole step
∨ = half step

The general rule for classifying major and minor intervals is that minor intervals have one half step less than that of major intervals of the same number.

◆ Diatonic Intervals • The Major Second

A **major second** is *an interval that is made up of one whole step.* Sing the following major seconds in the key of C major.

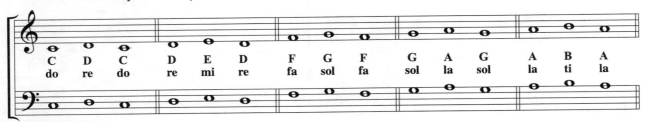

C	D	C	D	E	D	F	G	F	G	A	G	A	B	A
do	re	do	re	mi	re	fa	sol	fa	sol	la	sol	la	ti	la

◆ Practice

Sight-sing the following exercises to practice reading major seconds.

1 Key of G Major

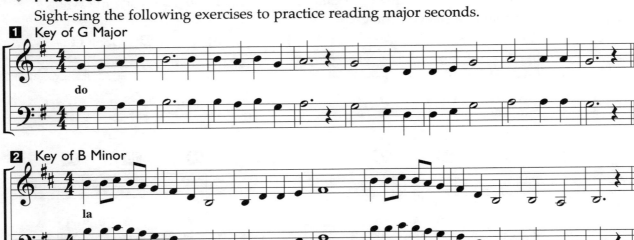

do

2 Key of B Minor

la

Pitch

◆ Diatonic Intervals • The Minor Second

A **minor second** is *an interval that is made up of one half step.* Sing the following minor seconds in the key of C major.

◆ Practice

Sight-sing the following exercises to practice reading major and minor seconds.

Pitch

◆ Diatonic Intervals • The Major Third

A **major third** is *an interval that is made up of two whole steps side by side.* Sing the following major thirds in the key of C major.

◆ Practice

Sight-sing the following exercises to practice reading major thirds.

Pitch

◆ Diatonic Intervals • The Minor Third

A **minor third** is *an interval that is made up of one whole step and one half step side by side.*
Sing the following minor thirds in the key of C major.

◆ Practice

Sight-sing the following exercises to practice reading minor thirds.

Practice

◆ Pitch and Rhythm • Diatonic Major and Minor Thirds

Using the patterns below as a guide, sight-sing the following exercises to practice reading major and minor thirds.

Pitch

◆ Diatonic Intervals • The Perfect Fourth

Diatonic intervals are *the relationships of the pitches that naturally occur within the scale of the key* (do, re, mi, fa, sol, la *and* ti). In some cases, instead of "major" or "minor," specific diatonic intervals are called "perfect." Octaves and primes are perfect intervals. Diatonic fourths and fifths are sometimes perfect intervals.

A **perfect fourth** is *an interval that is made up of two whole steps and one half step side by side.* Sing the following perfect fourths in the key of C major.

◆ Practice

Sight-sing the following exercises to practice reading perfect fourths.

Practice

◆ Pitch and Rhythm • Diatonic Perfect Fourths

Using the patterns below as a guide, sight-sing the following exercises to practice reading perfect fourths.

Pitch

◆ Diatonic Intervals • The Augmented Fourth and Diminished Fifth

Two further classifications of diatonic intervals are "augmented" and "diminished." An **augmented fourth** is *an interval that is made up of three whole steps side by side.* Sing the augmented fourth interval in the key of C major at the right.

A **diminished fifth** is *an interval that is made up of two whole steps and two half steps side by side.* Although the notes are written differently, the pitches of augmented fourth intervals and diminished fifth intervals sound the same because they are the same distance apart. Sing the diminished fifth interval in the key of C major at the right.

◆ Practice

Sight-sing the following exercises to practice reading augmented fourths and diminished fifths.

Pitch

◆ Diatonic Intervals • The Perfect Fifth

A **perfect fifth** is *an interval that is made up of three whole steps and one half step side by side.* Sing the following perfect fifths in the key of C major.

C	G	C	D	A	D	E	B	E	F	C	F	G	D	G	A	E	A
do	sol	do	re	la	re	mi	ti	mi	fa	do	fa	sol	re	sol	la	mi	la

◆ Practice

Sight-sing the following exercises to practice reading perfect fifths.

Practice

◆ Pitch and Rhythm • Diatonic Perfect Fifths

Using the patterns below as a guide, sight-sing the following exercises to practice reading perfect fifths.

Pitch

◆ Diatonic Intervals • The Major Sixth

A **major sixth** is *an interval that is made up of four whole steps and one half step side by side.* Sing the following major sixths in the key of C major.

◆ Practice

Sight-sing the following exercises to practice reading major sixths.

Pitch

◆ **Diatonic Intervals • The Minor Sixth**

A **minor sixth** is *an interval that is made up of three whole steps and two half steps side by side*. Sing the following minor sixths in the key of C major.

◆ **Practice**

Sight-sing the following exercises to practice reading minor sixths.

Practice

◆ Pitch and Rhythm • Diatonic Major and Minor Sixths

Using the patterns below as a guide, sight-sing the following exercises to practice reading major and minor sixths.

Pitch

◆ Diatonic Intervals • The Major Seventh

A **major seventh** is *an interval that is made up of five whole steps and one half step side by side.* Sing the following major sevenths in the key C major.

◆ Practice

Sight-sing the following exercises to practice reading major sevenths.

Pitch

◆ Diatonic Intervals • The Minor Seventh

A **minor seventh** is *an interval that is made up of four whole steps and two half steps side by side.* Sing the following minor sevenths in the key of C major.

D	C	D	E	D	E	G	F	G	A	G	A	B	A	B
re	do	re	mi	re	mi	sol	fa	sol	la	sol	la	ti	la	ti

◆ Practice

Sight-sing the following exercises to practice reading minor sevenths.

Practice

◆ Pitch and Rhythm • Diatonic Major and Minor Sevenths

Using the patterns below as a guide, sight-sing the following exercises to practice reading major and minor sevenths.

Pitch

◆ Diatonic Intervals • The Octave

An **octave** is *an interval that is made up of five whole steps and two half steps side by side.*
Sing the following octaves in the key of C major.

| C | C | C | D | D | D | E | E | E | F | F | F | G | G | G | A | A | A | B | B | B |
| do | do | do | re | re | re | mi | mi | mi | fa | fa | fa | sol | sol | sol | la | la | la | ti | ti | ti |

◆ Practice

Sight-sing the following exercises to practice reading octaves.

Evaluation

Demonstrate what you have learned in Chapter Three by completing the following:

◆ **True or False?**

1. An interval is the relationship of two pitches to a third pitch.

2. Diatonic intervals are the relationships of the pitches that naturally occur within the scale of the key.

◆ Identify the intervals in the following examples. Sing each interval.

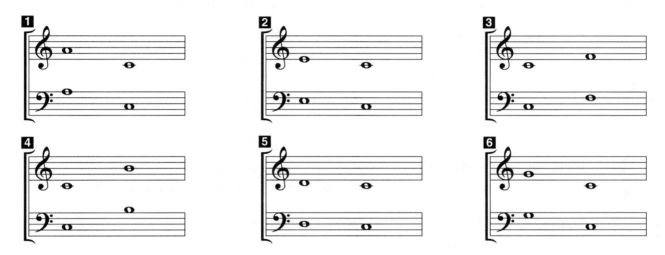

◆ Sight-sing the following melodies. In the boxed sets of notes, what intervals are being used?

CHAPTER 4

Rhythm

◆ Simple Meter • Division of the Beat

Simple meter is *any meter in which the beat is divisible by two.* $\frac{2}{4}$ meter is an example of simple meter since it has two beats in a measure with the quarter note receiving the beat.

2 = There are two beats per measure.
4 = The quarter note receives the beat. The division of the beat is the eighth note.

Common rhythm patterns in $\frac{2}{4}$ meter:

3 = There are three beats per measure.
4 = The quarter note receives the beat. The division of the beat is the eighth note.

Common rhythm patterns in $\frac{3}{4}$ meter:

4 = There are four beats per measure.
4 = The quarter note receives the beat. The division of the beat is the eighth note.

Common rhythm patterns in $\frac{4}{4}$ meter:

2 = There are two beats per measure.
2 = The half note receives the beat. The division of the beat is the quarter note.

Common rhythm patterns in $\frac{2}{2}$ meter:

$\frac{2}{2}$ meter is sometimes called "cut time" and is notated as ¢ .

3 = There are three beats per measure.
2 = The half note receives the beat. The division of the beat is the quarter note.

Common rhythm patterns in $\frac{3}{2}$ meter:

4 = There are four beats per measure.
2 = The half note receives the beat. The division of the beat is the quarter note.

Common rhythm patterns in $\frac{4}{2}$ meter:

2 = There are two beats per measure.
8 = The eighth note receives the beat. The division of the beat is the sixteenth note.

Common rhythm patterns in $\frac{2}{8}$ meter:

3 = There are three beats per measure.
8 = The eighth note receives the beat. The division of the beat is the sixteenth note.

Common rhythm patterns in $\frac{3}{8}$ meter:

4 = There are four beats per measure.
8 = The eighth note receives the beat. The division of the beat is the sixteenth note.

Common rhythm patterns in $\frac{4}{8}$ meter:

Rhythm

◆ Compound Meter • Division of the Beat

Compound meter is *any meter in which the beat is divided into multiples of three.* For example, $\frac{6}{8}$ meter is a compound meter since the beat is divided into two groups of three eighth notes each with two beats in a measure.

As in simple meters, compound meters are usually conducted in two, three or four, except when the tempo is very slow.

6 = The beat is divided into two groups of three eighth notes.

8 = The eighth note is the division. The dotted quarter note receives the beat (except in a very slow tempo).

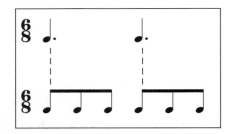
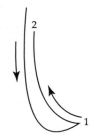

Common rhythm patterns in $\frac{6}{8}$ meter:

9 = The beat is divided into three groups of three eighth notes.

8 = The eighth note is the division. The dotted quarter note receives the beat (except in a very slow tempo)

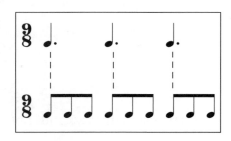
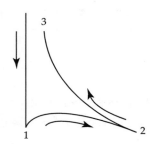

Common rhythm patterns in $\frac{9}{8}$ meter:

12 = The beat is divided into four groups of three eighth notes.
8 = The eighth note is the division. The dotted quarter note receives the beat.

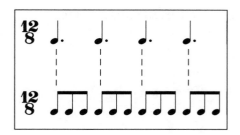

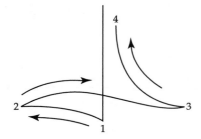

Common rhythm patterns in **12/8** meter:

Compound meter may be extended to meters in which the division is a note value other than an eighth note, such as **6/4**, **9/4** or **12/4**.

12 = The beat is divided into four groups of three quarter notes.
4 = The quarter note is the division. The dotted half note receives the beat.

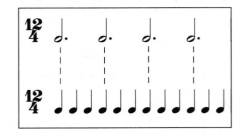

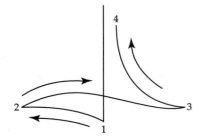

Common rhythm patterns in **12/4** meter:

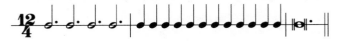

Practice

◆ Rhythm • Simple Meters

Clap, tap or chant while conducting the following exercises in simple meter.

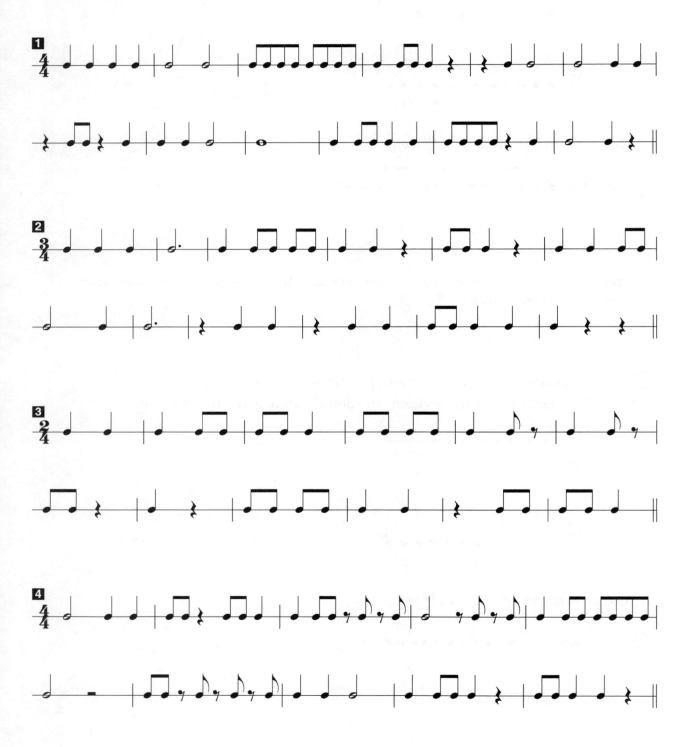

5

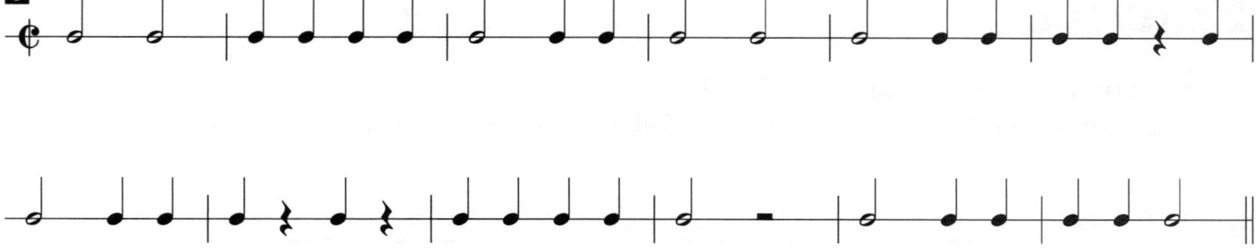

6

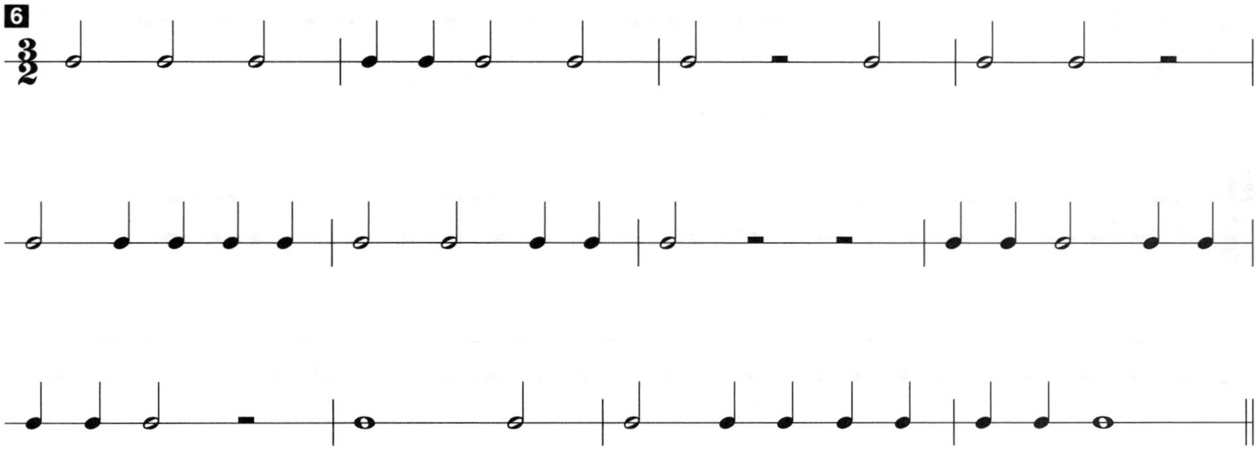

7

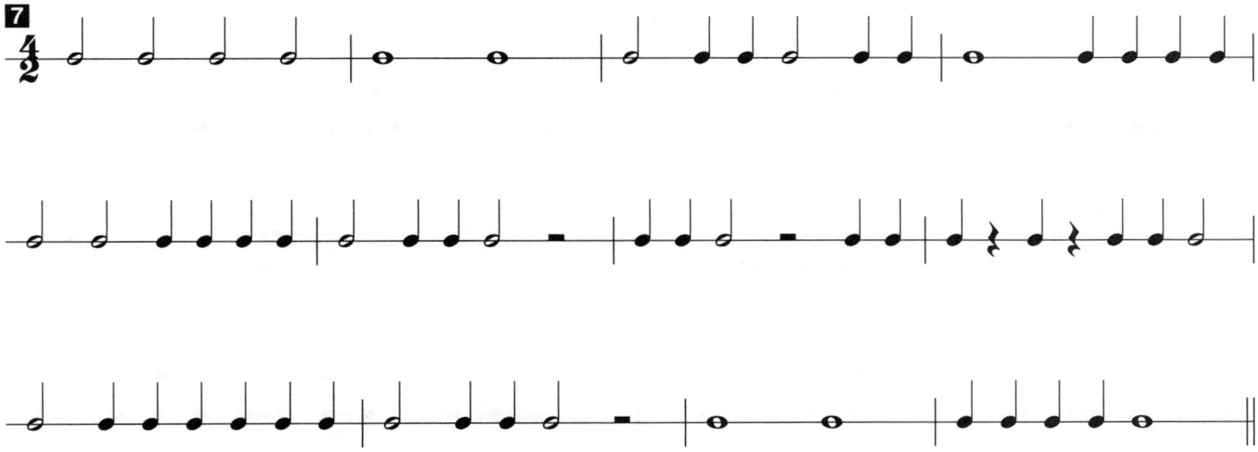

Practice

◆ Rhythm • Compound Meters
Clap, tap or chant while conducting the following exercises in compound meter.

Practice

◆ Rhythm • Less Common Meters

Clap, tap or chant while conducting the following exercises that are in meters which are less commonly used. Which are simple? Which are compound?

Rhythm

◆ Tied Notes

A **tie** is *a curved line used to connect two or more notes of the same pitch in order to make one longer note.*

◆ Practice

Clap, tap or chant while conducting the following exercises that use tied notes.

Rhythm

◆ Dotted Rhythms

A **dot** is *a symbol that increases the length of a given note by half its value.* It is placed to the right of the note.

When the quarter note receives the beat:

A dotted half note receives three beats (the same as a half note tied to a quarter note).

A dotted quarter note receives one and a half beats (the same as a quarter note tied to an eighth note).

Dotted rhythms are often combinations of unequal note values. For example, a longer dotted note is sometimes followed by a shorter note.

◆ Practice

Clap, tap or chant while conducting the following exercises that use dotted rhythms.

Practice

◆ Dotted Rhythms

Clap, tap or chant while conducting the following exercises that use dotted rhythms.

Advanced Sight-Singing *Chapter 4* **55**

Rhythm

◆ "Short-Long" Patterns
Sometimes a shorter note is followed by a longer dotted note.

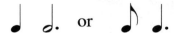

◆ Practice
Clap, tap or chant while conducting the following exercises that use "short-long" patterns.

Rhythm

◆ Rests

A note represents sound in music. A rest represents silence in music. For each note value, there is an equivalent rest.

◆ Whole Note and Whole Rest

When the quarter note receives the beat, a whole note represents four beats of sound and a whole rest represents four beats of silence.

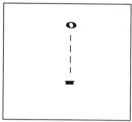

◆ Half Note and Half Rest

When the quarter note receives the beat, a half note represents two beats of sound and a half rest represents two beats of silence.

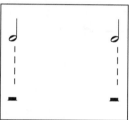

◆ Quarter Note and Quarter Rest

When the quarter note receives the beat, a quarter note represents one beat of sound and a quarter rest represents one beat of silence.

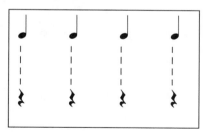

◆ Eighth Note and Eighth Rest

When the quarter note receives the beat, an eighth note represents half a beat of sound and an eighth rest represents half a beat of silence.

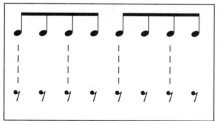

Practice

◆ Rhythm • Note and Rest Combinations

Clap, tap or chant while conducting the following exercises.

Evaluation

Demonstrate what you have learned in Chapter Four by completing the following:

◆ Identify the following time signatures as simple meter or compound meter.

$$\frac{3}{4} \quad \frac{12}{8} \quad \frac{4}{2} \quad \frac{2}{2} \quad \frac{9}{8} \quad \frac{4}{4} \quad \frac{4}{8} \quad \frac{12}{4} \quad \frac{3}{8}$$

◆ Musical Math

When the quarter note receives the beat, are the following equations true or false?

When the eighth note receives the beat, are the following equations true or false?

◆ Be A Composer

Create a rhythm composition of at least eight measures in either simple or compound meter using all notes and rests, along with tied and grouped notes appropriate for your meter choice.

◆ Challenge

Choose pitches for your rhythm composition and transfer your composition to a staff. Sing your melody using solfège syllables. Play your melody on a keyboard and/or create words for your melody.

CHAPTER 5

Pitch

◆ Altered Pitches

Sometimes, altered pitches are used in music. An **accidental** (another name for an altered pitch) is *any sharp, flat or natural that is not included in the key signature of a piece of music.* For example, in the key of C major, D♯ would be an altered pitch, or accidental.

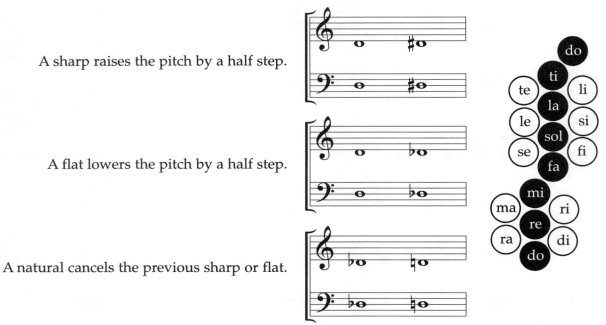

A sharp raises the pitch by a half step.

A flat lowers the pitch by a half step.

A natural cancels the previous sharp or flat.

◆ Chromatic Altered Pitches • *Di* and *Ra*

In any given key, if the first note of the scale, *do,* is altered by raising it a half step, the raised pitch is labeled *di.* If the second note of the scale, *re,* is altered by lowering it a half step, the lowered pitch is labeled *ra.*

On a keyboard, these two notes, *di* and *ra,* are the same pitch. For example, in the key of C major, C♯ *(di)* and D♭ *(ra)* are both played using the black key between C and D.

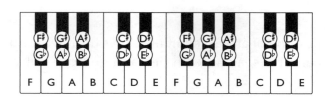

Practice

◆ **Pitch and Rhythm • *Di* and *Ra***
Sight-sing the following exercises.

Practice

◆ **Pitch and Rhythm • *Di* and *Ra***
Sight-sing the following exercises.

Pitch

◆ Chromatic Altered Pitches • *Ri* and *Ma*

In any given key, if the second note of the scale, *re*, is altered by raising it a half step, the raised pitch is labeled *ri*. If the third note of the scale, *mi*, is altered by lowering it a half step, the lowered pitch is labeled *ma*.

On a keyboard, these two notes, *ri* and *ma*, are the same pitch. For example, in the key of C major, D♯ (*ri*) and E♭ (*ma*) are both played by using the black key between D and E.

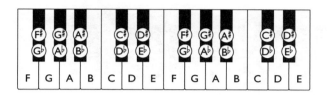

◆ Practice

Sight-sing the following exercises.

Pitch

◆ Chromatic Altered Pitches • *Fi* and *Se*

In any given key, if the fourth note of the scale, *fa*, is altered by raising it a half step, the raised pitch is labeled *fi*. If the fifth note of the scale, *sol*, is altered by lowering it a half step, the lowered pitch is labeled *se*.

On a keyboard, these two notes, *fi* and *se*, are the same pitch. For example, in the key of C major, F♯ *(fi)* and G♭ *(se)* are both played by using the black key between F and G.

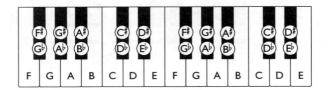

◆ Practice

Sight-sing the following exercises.

Pitch

◆ Chromatic Altered Pitches • *Si* and *Le*

In any given key, if the fifth note of the scale, *sol*, is altered by raising it a half step, the raised pitch is labeled *si*. If the sixth note of the scale, *la*, is altered by lowering it a half step, the lowered pitch is labeled *le*.

On a keyboard, these two notes, *si* and *la*, are the same pitch. For example, in the key of C major, G♯ *(si)* and A♭ *(le)* are both played by using the black key between G and A.

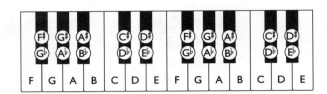

◆ Practice

Sight-sing the following exercises.

Pitch

◆ Chromatic Altered Pitches • *Li* and *Te*

In any given key, if the sixth note of the scale, *la*, is altered by raising it a half step, the raised pitch is labeled *li*. If the seventh note of the scale, *ti*, is altered by lowering it a half step, the lowered pitch is labeled *te*.

On a keyboard, these two notes, *li* and *te*, are the same pitch. For example, in the key of C major, A♯ *(li)* and B♭ *(te)* are both played by using the black key between A and B.

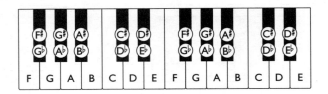

◆ Practice

Sight-sing the following exercises.

Evaluation

Demonstrate what you have learned in Chapter Five by completing the following:

◆ **Review Chromatic Scales**
Using solfège syllables, sing the chromatic scale ascending and descending.

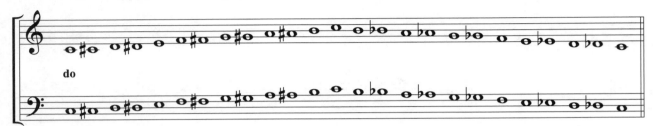

◆ Sight-sing the following exercises. Name the key of each exercise.

CHAPTER 6

Rhythm

◆ Simple Meter • Division and Subdivision of the Beat

Simple meter is *any meter in which the beat is divisible by two.* $\frac{2}{4}$ meter is an example of simple meter since it has two beats in a measure with the quarter note receiving the beat.

2 = There are two beats per measure.
4 = The quarter note receives the beat. The division of the beat is the eighth note. The subdivision of the beat is the sixteenth note.

Common rhythm patterns in $\frac{2}{4}$ meter:

3 = There are three beats per measure.
4 = The quarter note receives the beat. The division of the beat is the eighth note. The subdivision of the beat is the sixteenth note.

Common rhythm patterns in $\frac{3}{4}$ meter:

4 = There are four beats per measure.
4 = The quarter note receives the beat. The division of the beat is the eighth note. The subdivision of the beat is the sixteenth note.

Common rhythm patterns in $\frac{4}{4}$ meter:

2 = There are two beats per measure.
2 = The half note receives the beat. The division of the beat is the quarter note. The subdivision of the beat is the eighth note.

Common rhythm patterns in $\frac{2}{2}$ meter:

$\frac{2}{2}$ is sometimes called "cut time" and is notated as ¢.

Rhythm

◆ Simple Meter • Division and Subdivision of the Beat

3
2
= There are three beats per measure.
= The half note receives the beat. The division of the beat is the quarter note. The subdivision of the beat is the eighth note.

Common rhythm patterns in ¾ meter:

4
2
= There are four beats per measure.
= The half note receives the beat. The division of the beat is the quarter note. The subdivision of the beat is the eighth note.

Common rhythm patterns in ⁴⁄₂ meter:

2
8
= There are two beats per measure.
= The eighth note receives the beat. The division of the beat is the sixteenth note. The subdivision of the beat is a three-beamed note called a 32nd note.

Common rhythm patterns in ²⁄₈ meter:

3
8
= There are three beats per measure.
= The eighth note receives the beat. The division of the beat is the sixteenth note. The subdivision of the beat is the 32nd note.

Common rhythm patterns in ⅜ meter:

4
8
= There are four beats per measure.
= The eighth note receives the beat. The division of the beat is the sixteenth note. The subdivision of the beat is the 32nd note.

Common rhythm patterns in ⁴⁄₈ meter:

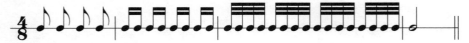

Rhythm

◆ Compound Meter • Division and Subdivision of the Beat

Compound meter is *any meter in which the beat is divided into multiples of three.* For example, $\frac{6}{8}$ meter is a compound meter since the beat is divided into two groups of three eighth notes, each with two beats in a measure.

As in simple meters, compound meters are usually conducted in two, three or four, except when the tempo is very slow.

6 = The beat is divided into two groups of three eighth notes.

8 = The eighth note is the division. The dotted quarter receives the beat (except in a very slow tempo). The eighth note can be subdivided into sixteenth notes.

Common rhythm patterns in $\frac{6}{8}$ meter:

9 = The beat is divided into three groups of three eighth notes.

8 = The eighth note is the division. The dotted quarter receives the beat (except in a very slow tempo). The eighth note can be subdivided into sixteenth notes.

Common rhythm patterns in $\frac{9}{8}$ meter:

Rhythm

◆ Compound Meter • Division and Subdivision of the Beat

12 = The beat is divided into four groups of three eighth notes each.
8 = The eighth note is the division. The dotted quarter receives the beat. The eighth note can be subdivided into sixteenth notes.

Common rhythm patterns in $\frac{12}{8}$ meter:

Compound meter may be extended to meters in which the division is a value other than an eighth note, such as $\frac{6}{4}$, $\frac{9}{4}$ or $\frac{12}{4}$.

6 = The beat is divided into two groups of three quarter notes each.
4 = The quarter note is the division. The dotted half receives the beat (except in a very slow tempo). The quarter note can be subdivided into eighth notes.

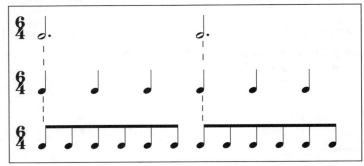

Common rhythm patterns in $\frac{6}{4}$ meter:

Practice

◆ Rhythm • Simple Meters
Clap, tap or chant while conducting the following exercises in simple meter.

Practice

◆ Rhythm • Simple Meters
Clap, tap or chant while conducting the following exercises in simple meter.

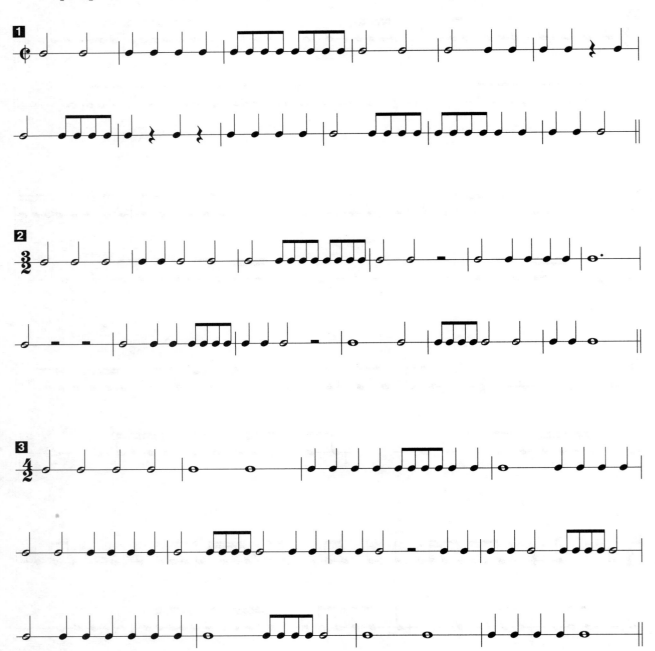

Practice

◆ Rhythm • Compound Meters

Clap, tap or chant while conducting the following exercises in compound meter.

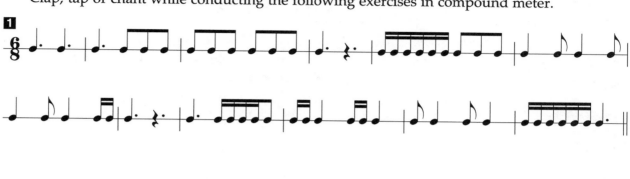

Practice

◆ Rhythm • Less Common Meters

Clap, tap or chant while conducting the following exercises in meters that are less commonly used. Which are simple? Which are compound?

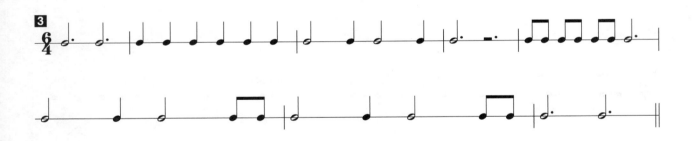

Rhythm

◆ More Tied Notes

A **tie** is *a curved line used to connect two or more notes of the same pitch in order to make one longer note.*

◆ Practice

Clap, tap or chant while conducting the following exercises that use tied notes.

Rhythm

◆ More Dotted Rhythms

A **dot** is *a symbol that increases the length of a given note by half its value.* It is placed to the right of the note.

When the quarter note receives the beat:

A dotted half note receives three beats (the same as a half note tied to a quarter note).

A dotted quarter note receives one and a half beats (the same as a quarter note tied to an eighth note).

A dotted eighth note receives three-fourths of a beat (the same as an eighth note tied to an sixteenth note).

Dotted rhythms are often combinations of unequal note values. For example, a longer dotted note is sometimes followed by a shorter note.

◆ Practice

Clap, tap or chant while conducting the following exercises that use dotted rhythms.

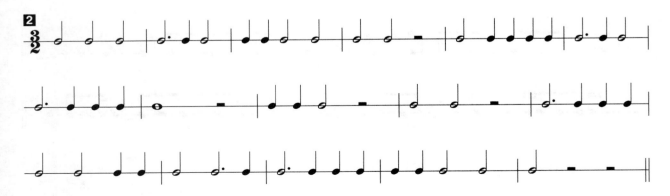

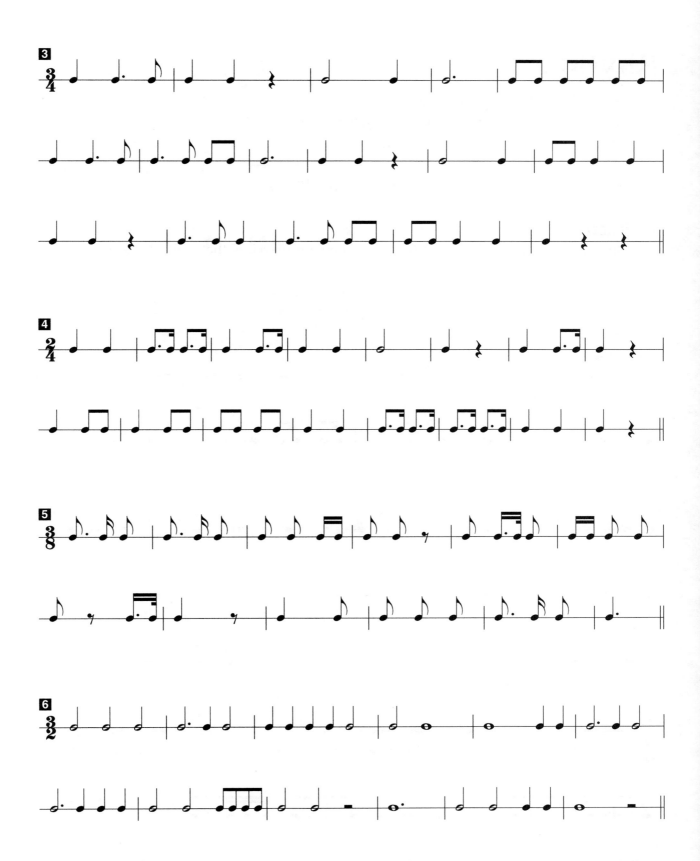

Rhythm

◆ More "Short-Long" Patterns

Sometimes a shorter note is followed by a longer dotted note.

◆ Practice

Clap, tap or chant while conducting the following exercises that use "short-long" patterns.

Rhythm

◆ More About Rests

A note represents sound in music. A rest represents silence in music. For each note value, there is an equivalent rest.

Whole Note and Whole Rest
When the quarter note receives the beat, a whole note represents four beats of sound and a whole rest represents four beats of silence.

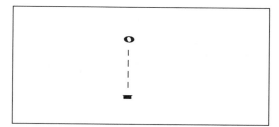

Half Note and Half Rest
When the quarter note receives the beat, a half note represents two beats of sound and a half rest represents two beats of silence.

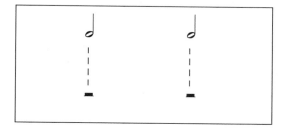

Quarter Note and Quarter Rest
When the quarter note receives the beat, a quarter note represents one beat of sound and a quarter rest represents one beat of silence.

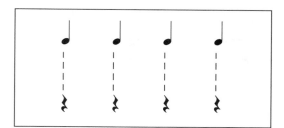

Eighth Note and Eighth Rest
When the quarter note receives the beat, an eighth note represents half a beat of sound and an eighth rest represents half a beat of silence.

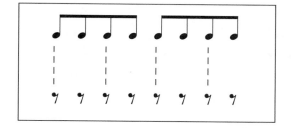

Sixteenth Note and Sixteenth Rest
When the quarter note receives the beat, a sixteenth note represents one quarter beat of sound and a sixteenth rest represents one quarter beat of silence.

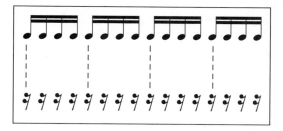

Practice

◆ Rhythm • More Note and Rest Combinations

Clap, tap or chant while conducting the following exercises.

4

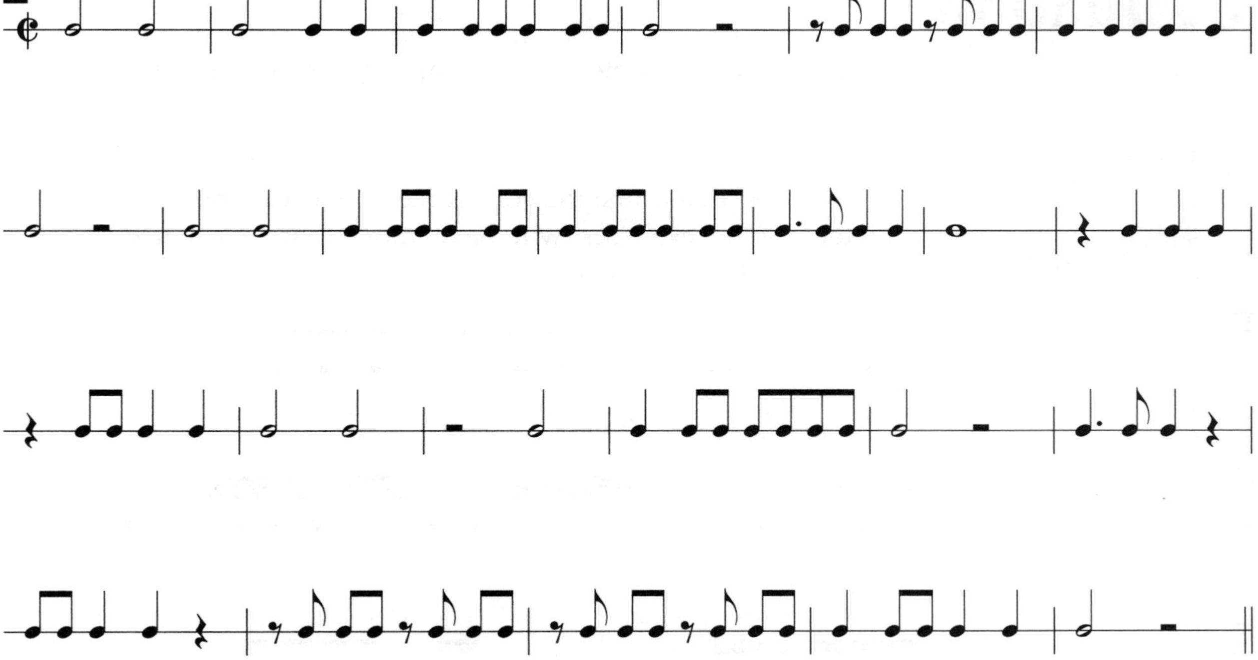

5

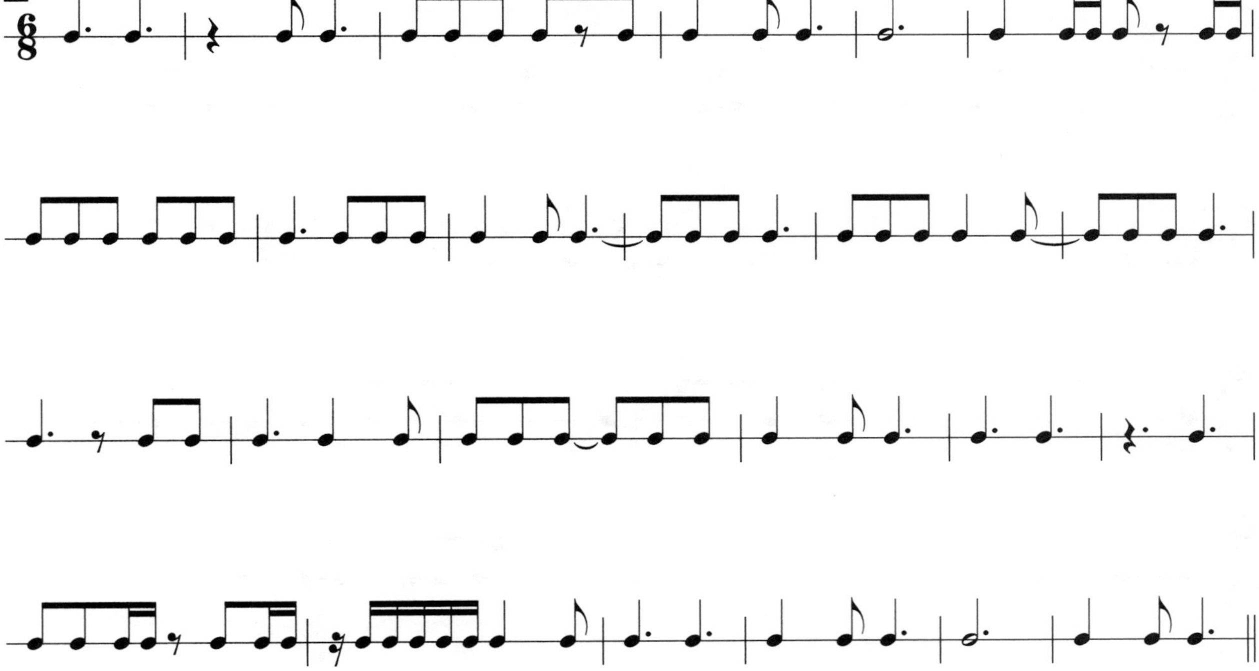

Evaluation

Demonstrate what you have learned in Chapter Six by completing the following:

◆ Mystery Meters

For each of the following exercises, determine the correct meter and whether it is a simple or compound meter. (Some exercises will have more than one correct answer.) Then clap, tap or chant while conducting each exercise.

CHAPTER 7

Pitch

◆ Diatonic Intervals

An **interval** is *the relationship of one note to another.* **Diatonic intervals** are *the relationships of the notes that naturally occur within the scale of the key* (do, re, mi, fa, sol, la *and* ti). The interval from one note to another is given a number, depending upon the distance between the two notes. For example, the distance from *do* to *mi* is called a "third" (3rd) because *do* and *mi* are three notes apart (*do, re* and *mi*).

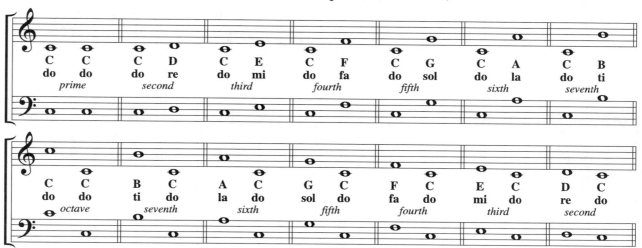

◆ Non-Diatonic Intervals

Non-diatonic intervals are *the relationships of the notes that do not occur naturally within the scale of the key.* In other words, they include notes which have been chromatically altered (sharps, flats and naturals.) As with diatonic intervals, non-diatonic intervals are given a number, depending upon the distance between the two notes.

Below are three examples of non-diatonic intervals in the key of C major.

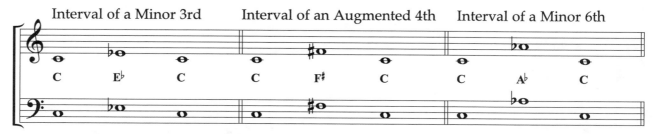

Since solfège syllables are used almost exclusively as tools in sight-reading diatonic music, they are not included in the presentation of the non-diatonic interval drills in this chapter. While practicing these intervals in the following charts, sing using the neutral syllable "loo". However, it is very appropriate to use solfège syllables to read the melodic exercises in this chapter.

Pitch

◆ Non-Diatonic Intervals • The Major Second

A **major second** is *an interval that is made up of one whole step.* Sing the following non-diatonic major seconds in the key of C major.

C♯ D♯ C♯   D♯ E♯ D♯   E   F♯ E   F♯ G♯ F♯   G♯ A♯ G♯   A♯ B♯ A♯   B C♯ B

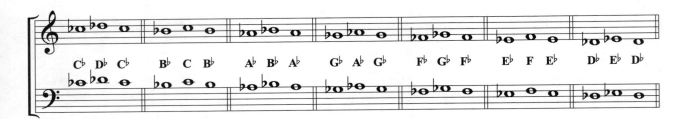

C♭ D♭ C♭   B♭ C B♭   A♭ B♭ A♭   G♭ A♭ G♭   F♭ G♭ F♭   E♭ F E♭   D♭ E♭ D♭

◆ Practice

Sight-sing the following exercises to practice reading non-diatonic major seconds.

1 Key of G Major

do

2 Key of F Major

sol

Pitch

◆ Non-Diatonic Intervals • The Minor Second

A **minor second** is *an interval that is made up of one half step.* Sing the following non-diatonic minor seconds in the key of C major.

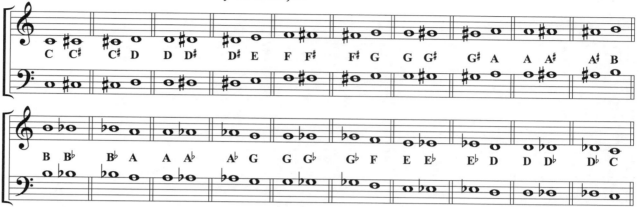

◆ Practice

Sight-sing the following exercises to practice reading non-diatonic minor seconds.

Practice

◆ **Pitch and Rhythm • Non-Diatonic Major and Minor Seconds**
Sight-sing the following exercises to practice reading non-diatonic major and minor seconds.

Pitch

◆ Non-Diatonic Intervals • The Major Third

A **major third** is *an interval that is made up of two whole steps side by side.* Sing the following non-diatonic major thirds in the key of C major.

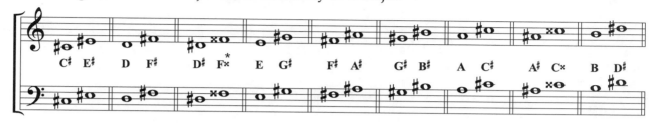

C♯ E♯   D F♯   D♯ F𝄪*   E G♯   F♯ A♯   G♯ B♯   A C♯   A♯ C𝄪   B D♯

E♭ C♭   D B♭   D♭ B♭♭†   C A♭   B♭ G♭   A♭ F♭   G E♭   G♭ E♭♭   F D♭

* A double sharp (𝄪) is a symbol that raises a given pitch two half steps.
† A double flat (♭♭) is a symbol that lowers a given pitch two half steps.

◆ Practice

Sight-sing the following exercises to practice reading non-diatonic major thirds.

1   Key of D Major

     do

2   Key of F Major

     do

3   Key of B Minor

     la

Pitch

◆ **Non-Diatonic Intervals • The Minor Third**

A **minor third** is *an interval that is made up of one whole step and one half step side by side.*
Sing the following non-diatonic minor thirds in the key of C major.

◆ **Practice**

Sight-sing the following exercises to practice reading non-diatonic minor thirds.

Practice

◆ **Pitch and Rhythm • Non-Diatonic Major and Minor Thirds**

Sight-sing the following exercises to practice reading non-diatonic major and minor thirds.

Pitch

◆ Non-Diatonic Intervals • The Perfect Fourth

A **perfect fourth** is *an interval that is made up of two whole steps and one half step side by side.* Sing the following non-diatonic perfect fourths in the key of C major.

◆ Practice

Sight-sing the following exercises to practice reading non-diatonic perfect fourths.

Practice

◆ **Pitch and Rhythm • Non-Diatonic Perfect Fourths**
Sight-sing the following exercises to practice reading non-diatonic perfect fourths.

Pitch

◆ Non-Diatonic Intervals • The Augmented Fourth

An **augmented fourth** is *an interval that is made up of three whole steps side by side.* Sing the following non-diatonic augmented fourths in the key of C major.

C F# C   Db G Db   D G# D   Eb A Eb   E A# E   F# B# F#   G C# G   Ab D Ab   A D# A   Bb E Bb

◆ Practice

Sight-sing the following exercises to practice reading non-diatonic augmented fourths.

Pitch

◆ Non-Diatonic Intervals • The Diminished Fifth

A **diminished fifth** is *an interval that is made up of two whole steps and two half steps side by side.* Sing the following non-diatonic diminished fifths in the key of C major.

C G♭ C   C♯ G C♯   D A♭ D   D♯ A D♯   E B♭ E   F♯ C F♯   G D♭ G   G♯ D G♯   A E♭ A   A♯ E A♯

◆ Practice

Sight-sing the following exercises to practice reading non-diatonic diminished fifths.

1 Key of C Major

2 Key of A Major

3 Key of G Major

4 Key of E Minor

5 Key of C Minor

Practice

◆ Pitch and Rhythm • Non-Diatonic Augmented Fourths and Diminished Fifths

Sight-sing the following exercises to practice reading non-diatonic augmented fourths and diminished fifths.

Pitch

◆ Non-Diatonic Intervals • The Perfect Fifth

A **perfect fifth** is *an interval that is made up of three whole steps and one half step side by side.* Sing the following non-diatonic perfect fifths in the key of C major.

◆ Practice

Sight-sing the following exercises to practice reading non-diatonic perfect fifths.

Practice

◆ Pitch and Rhythm • Non-Diatonic Perfect Fifths

Sight-sing the following exercises to practice reading non-diatonic perfect fifths.

Pitch

◆ Non-Diatonic Intervals • The Major Sixth

A **major sixth** is *an interval that is made up of four whole steps and one half step side by side.* Sing the following non-diatonic major sixths in the key of C major.

◆ Practice

Sight-sing the following exercises to practice reading non-diatonic major sixths.

Pitch

◆ Non-Diatonic Intervals • The Minor Sixth

A **minor sixth** is *an interval that is made up of three whole steps and two half steps side by side.* Sing the following non-diatonic minor sixths in the key of C major.

◆ Practice

Sight-sing the following exercises to practice reading non-diatonic minor sixths.

Practice

◆ ## Pitch and Rhythm • Non-Diatonic Major and Minor Sixths

Sight-sing the following exercises to practice reading non-diatonic major and minor sixths.

Pitch

◆ Non-Diatonic Intervals • The Major Seventh

A **major seventh** is *an interval that is made up of five whole steps and one half step side by side.* Sing the following non-diatonic major sevenths in the key of C major.

◆ Practice

Sight-sing the following exercises to practice reading non-diatonic major sevenths.

Pitch

◆ Non-Diatonic Intervals • The Minor Seventh

A **minor seventh** is *an interval that is made up of four whole steps and two half steps side by side.* Sing the following non-diatonic minor sevenths in the key of C major.

◆ Practice

Sight-sing the following exercises to practice reading non-diatonic minor sevenths.

1 Key of F Major

do

2 Key of B♭ Major

do

3 Key of G Minor

la

4 Key of D Minor

la

Practice

◆ Pitch and Rhythm • Non-Diatonic Major and Minor Sevenths

Sight-sing the following exercises to practice reading non-diatonic major and minor sevenths.

Pitch

◆ Non-Diatonic Intervals • The Octave

An **octave** is *an interval that is made up of five whole steps and two halfs steps.* Sing the following non-diatonic octaves in the key of C major.

◆ Practice

Sight-sing the following exercises to practice reading non-diatonic octaves.

Evaluation

Demonstrate what you have learned in Chapter Seven by completing the following:

◆ Vocabulary

Choose the best answer for the definitions below.

Non-Diatonic Interval   Non-Diatonic Diminished Fifth   Non-Diatonic Major Third

Prime   Octave

1. An interval that is five whole steps and two half steps side by side.
2. Two whole steps side by side using pitches that do not naturally occur in a given key.
3. Two whole steps and two half steps side by side using pitches that do not naturally occur in a given key.
4. A repeated tonic note.
5. The relationship of notes that do not occur naturally in a given key.

◆ Sight-sing the following exercise. In the boxed sets of notes, what intervals are being used?

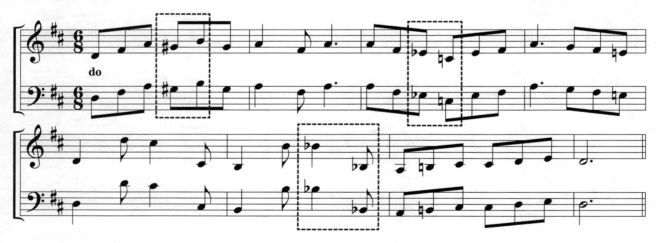

◆ Challenge

Conduct the above exercise as you sing.

CHAPTER 8

Rhythm

◆ Mixed Meter

Sometimes meters will change within a piece of music. When this happens, the number of beats per measure will change based on the top number of the meter signature.

In $\frac{2}{4}$, $\frac{3}{4}$ and $\frac{4}{4}$ meters, the quarter note beat remains the same, but the number of beats per measure changes.

◆ Practice

In the exercise below, keep the beat steady and practice conducting as you clap, tap or chant the the rhythm.

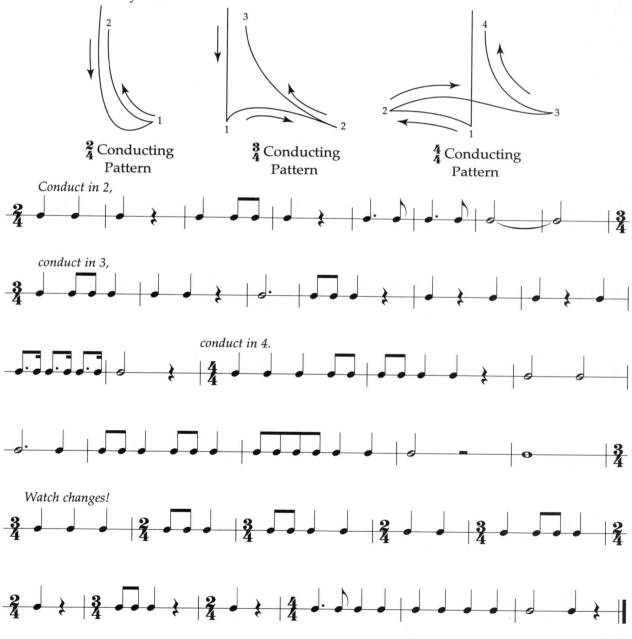

Practice

◆ Rhythm • Mixed Meter

Clap, tap or chant while conducting the following exercises to practice reading rhythms in mixed meter. Always keep the beat steady.

Rhythm

◆ More About Mixed Meter

When the meter changes, the beat can either change or remain constant. For example, when the meter changes from $\frac{4}{4}$ to ¢ the beat can change from the quarter note to the half note or the quarter note can remain constant. Notice the direction given in the parentheses below. Clap, tap or chant while conducting the following exercises.

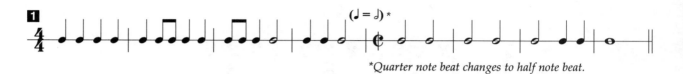

Quarter note beat changes to half note beat.

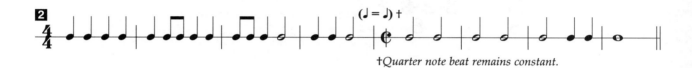

†*Quarter note beat remains constant.*

When the meter changes from simple to compound meter, either the beat can remain constant or the division can remain constant. Notice the direction given in the parentheses below.

Beat remains constant.

†*Eighth note division remains constant.*

Rhythm

◆ Asymmetrical Meters

Asymmetrical meter is *any meter in which the strong beats create combinations of twos and three*. Here are some examples of asymmetrical meters.

$$\frac{5}{4} = \frac{3+2}{4} \quad or \quad \frac{2+3}{4}$$

$$\frac{7}{8} = \frac{2+2+3}{8} \quad or \quad \frac{2+3+2}{8} \quad or \quad \frac{3+2+2}{8}$$

$$\frac{11}{8} = \frac{3+3+3+2}{8} \quad \text{(and several other combinations)}$$

◆ Practice

Clap, tap or chant while conducting the following exercises in asymmetrical meters.

Practice

◆ Rhythm • Mixed and Asymmetrical Meters

Clap, tap or chant while conducting the following exercises in mixed and asymmetrical meters.

Practice

◆ Rhythm • Mixed and Asymmetrical Meters

Clap, tap or chant while conducting the following exercises in mixed and asymmetrical meters.

Rhythm

◆ Triplets and Duplets

Simple meter is *any meter in which the beat is divisible by two.* $\frac{2}{4}$, $\frac{3}{4}$ and $\frac{4}{4}$ are examples of simple meter, as the quarter note receives the beat.

Compound meter is *any meter in which the beat is divided into multiples of three.* $\frac{6}{8}$ is an example of compound meter, as the dotted quarter note receives the beat, except in a very slow tempo.

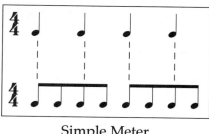

Simple Meter   Compound Meter

Sometimes in simple meter, there is a need for the beat to be divided into three. Likewise, in compound meter, the beat sometimes is divided into two. This is called borrowed division of the beat.

The borrowed division in simple meter is called a triplet, or a borrowed division of three where two would normally be. The borrowed division in compound meter is called a duplet, or a borrowed division of two where three would normally be.

See the following examples and observe how this is notated with a bracket over the borrowed grouping of notes. Sometimes there is no bracket, only a number.

◆ Practice

Clap, tap or chant while conducting the following exercises with triplets and duplets. Keep the beat steady.

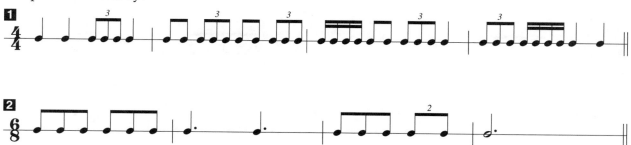

Rhythm

◆ More About Triplets and Duplets

Any note value can be a triplet or duplet. Here are some other examples.

◆ Quarter Note Triplets

In simple meter, a quarter note triplet occupies the same amount of time as two quarter notes or one half note. Practice the following patterns until you can perform the quarter note triplet evenly.

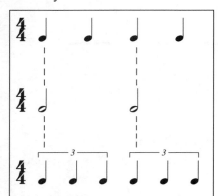

◆ Half Note Triplets

In simple meter, a half note triplet occupies the same amount of time as two half notes or one whole note. Practice the following patterns until you can perform the half note triplet evenly.

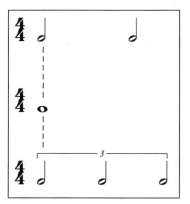

◆ Practice

Clap, tap or chant while conducting the following exercises that use triplets and duplets.

Evaluation

Demonstrate what you have learned in Chapter Eight by completing the following:

◆ Be A Conductor

Form small groups. Using the rhythm exercises below, select one person to conduct the exercises while the others tap or clap the rhythms. Take turns so each person has the chance to conduct.

◆ Be A Composer

Using at least one example of the rhythm concepts listed below, compose a rhythm composition of at least 32 measures.

- Any simple meter
- Any compound meter
- Include changing meter measures
- Beat directions during changing meter measures
- An example of asymmetrical meter
- Triplet or duplet rhythm configuration of notes in a measure

◆ Challenge

Add pitch to your composition using chromatic alteration in some way. Play and sing your composition.

CHAPTER 9

Pitch

◆ Common Chord Modulation • Relative Major and Minor Keys

Modulation is *the process of changing the tonality or the key of a piece of music.* It is one of the most common ways in which composers provide harmonic variety in their music. The simplest form of modulation is between relative major and minor keys.

The exercise below begins in F major and modulates to its relative minor key, D minor. Sight-sing this exercise and note that the tonality of the music changes from the key of F major to that of D minor.

◆ Common Chord Modulation • Pivot Chords

When modulation occurs between keys other than relative major and minor, it may be done through the use of a **pivot chord** (sometimes called a common chord), which is *a chord that is common to both the old and the new key.*

Play on the piano, or using the neutral syllable "loo" slowly sing the example below. The pivot chord, tonic (I) in C major, also functions as the subdominiant (IV) chord in G major, which is the new key.

To identify the pivot chord in a piece of music, find the chord that no longer functions in the first key. Usually the pivot chord is the one that immediately precedes this chord.

Practice

◆ Pitch and Rhythm • Common Chord Modulation

In the example below, identify the chord functions of each chord in the first key (B♭ major) from the beginning through the pivot chord, and then identify the chord functions in the second key (F major) beginning at the pivot chord and continuing on to the end. The first and last chords have been done for you.

Pivot Chord

◆ Practice

Sight-sing the exercise below. To sight-sing with solfège syllables through a modulation, make the change of syllables from one tonality to the next at the pivot chord. The exercise below is an open-score version of the example above. Sing this exercise, noting that the solfège syllables shift to the new tonality beginning at the pivot chord.

Pitch

◆ Diatonic Common Chord Modulation

A further way to describe common chord modulation is to call it **diatonic chord modulation.** This is simply a way to indicate that *all of the notes of the pivot chord are common, or with no altered pitches, in both the old and new keys.*

In each exercise below, determine the beginning tonality and the ending tonality. Find the pivot chord and determine which syllable to sing there. (Remember that to identify the pivot chord, find the chord that no longer functions in the first key. Usually the pivot chord is the one that immediately precedes this chord.) Then sight-sing each exercise below to practice diatonic common chord modulation.

Break Forth, O Beauteous Heav'nly Light

J. S. Bach

Pitch

◆ Common Tone Modulation

Like common chord modulation, modulation may also be done through the use of a **pivot tone** (sometimes called a common tone), that is *a tone that is common to both the old and new keys.* To identify the pivot tone in a piece of music, find the tone that no longer functions in the first key. Usually the pivot tone is the one that immediately precedes this note.

Pivot Tone

◆ Practice

For the following exercises, first identify the beginning tonality and the ending tonality. Find the pivot tone and determine which solfège syllable to sing there. Then sight-sing the exercise to practice common tone modulation.

Practice

◆ Pitch and Rhythm • Common Tone Modulation

Because the common tone to both the old and new key is a non-altered note, common tone modulation is also referred to as diatonic tone modulation.

For each of the following exercises, first identify the beginning tonality and the ending tonality. Find the pivot tone and determine which solfège syllable to sing there. Then sight-sing each exercise to practice common tone modulation.

* to melodic minor

Pitch

◆ Chromatic Modulation

Another way in which a change in tonality occurs in music is by **chromatic modulation,** which is made through *the use of a chord that is chromatically altered in either the old key or both the old and the new key.* In chromatic modulation, there is no common chord to function as the bridge between the two keys.

In the example below, the modulation begins with the third chord, which is chromatically altered in the key of G. Play, or using the neutral syllable "loo", sing this example, studying the chord functions. Note that there is no common chord to both the old and new keys.

* This chord does not function diatonically in the old key of G major.

** This chord does not function diatonically in the new key of E♭ major.

◆ Practice

To perform a chromatic modulation using solfège syllables, make the change of tonality beginning at the first chord that functions in the new key. When sight-singing, by looking ahead in the music, make the change as soon as possible when noting the shift in the tonality. The exercise below is an open-score version of the example above. Sing this exercise, noting where the solfège syllables shift to the new tonality.

Practice

◆ Pitch and Rhythm • Chromatic Modulation

For each exercise below, first identify the beginning tonality and the ending tonality. Find the altered pitch that signals the modulation and determine which solfège syllable to sing there. Then sight-sing the exercise to practice chromatic modulation.

Pitch

◆ Enharmonic Modulation

Enharmonic notes are *notes that appear differently on a page of music, but whose pitches sound the same.* For example, A♭ and G♯ are enharmonic notes. **Enharmonic modulation** *involves the enharmonic change of one or more notes during the process of moving from the old key to the new key.*

Below, the modulation begins with the chromatically-altered D♭ in the second measure. This is an example of an enharmonic modulation because the D♭ is tied to the C♯ in the following measure. The pitch remains the same, but the notes (D♭ and C♯) are different. Play, or using the neutral syllable "loo", sing this example.

To perform an enharmonic modulation using solfège syllables, make the change of tonality on the second enharmonic note, as indicated in the second example below.

Begin in F Major   End in D Major

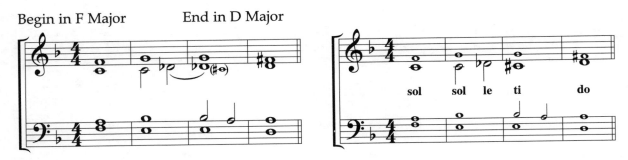

◆ Practice

Sight-sing the following exercise to practice enharmonic modulation. Bass clef singers, change the solfège syllables from the old key to the new key where the treble clef singers do, at the *.

Practice

◆ Pitch and Rhythm • Multiple Modulations

Challenge. Sight-sing the following melody which modulates several times.

Modulation Maze

Evaluation

Demonstrate what you have learned in Chapter Nine by completing the following:

◆ Modulation Methods

Study each of the following exercises that modulate. Using the different modulation types listed below, identify which type best describes each exercise. Then sight-sing each exercise.

Common Chord Modulation   Enharmonic Modulation

Chromatic Modulation

◆ Challenge

Locate the pivot chord in the common chord exercise.

CHAPTER 10

Pitch

◆ Polytonal and Atonal Melodies

Music that modulates frequently or is without a fixed key is common in music written from the late nineteenth century onward. To sight-sing this type of music, the use of fixed *do* is common.

In fixed *do*, *do* is always C, and the pitch syllables are always the same, no matter what key or key feeling of the music.

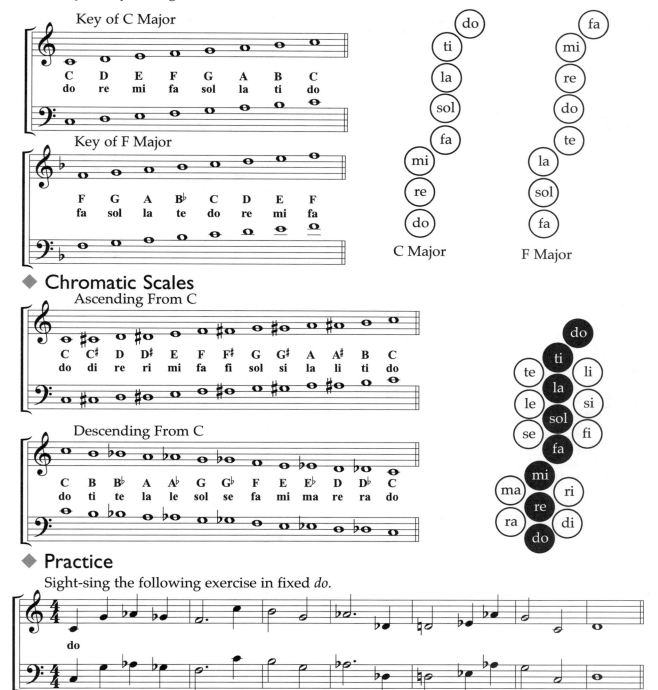

◆ Chromatic Scales

◆ Practice

Sight-sing the following exercise in fixed *do*.

Practice

◆ **Pitch and Rhythm • Polytonal and Atonal Melodies**
Sight-sing the following exercises using fixed *do*.

Practice

◆ Pitch and Rhythm • Polytonal and Atonal Melodies

Sight-sing the following exercises using fixed *do*.

Evaluation

Demonstrate what you have learned in Chapter Ten by completing the following:

◆ Fixed *Do* Challenge

Name the notes below using fixed *do*. Sing the pitches using fixed *do*.

◆ Be A Composer

Copy the following rhythm pattern onto a separate sheet of paper. Assign a fixed *do* pitch to each note. Transfer your melody to the staff and practice singing or playing your melody on a keyboard or other melody instrument.

Appendix

To The Teacher

EXPERIENCING CHORAL MUSIC–Advanced Sight-Singing is designed to provide a sequential program to be used in the choral classroom for the study of music theory and music reading skills. For students to gain the most from this material, plan 10–15 minutes of daily study, including the introduction of new material, as well as the practice and review of previous material.

◆ Features of the Program
- The sequence is pedagogically sound and practical.
- The terminology is accurate and literal.
- Music theory is presented in a format that is compatible with the material in the *EXPERIENCING CHORAL MUSIC* repertoire books. Cross-references are provided in each repertoire book to the coordinating concepts in this book.
- It is designed to be successful within a variety of choral organizations: treble, tenor/bass or mixed.

How To Use This Book

EXPERIENCING CHORAL MUSIC–Advanced Sight-Singing is organized into 10 chapters that include material for developing skills in music theory, sight-singing melodic exercises and sight-reading rhythmic exercises. Each chapter concludes with a comprehensive evaluation.

◆ Sight-Singing
The sight-singing exercises are designed to allow students to practice the concepts presented in each chapter. Included in this material are:
- Various musical terms and symbols.
- The use of solfège syllables to identify and sing correct pitches.

◆ Methods of Sight-Singing
There are many good methods to use in developing sight-singing skills. For the melodic exercises, consider using numbers or solfège syllables (movable or fixed *do*). For rhythm reading, consider the Eastman, Traditional or Kodály methods. It is important to be consistent and use the same method daily. More information about each method is included in this Appendix.

National Standards High School Grades 9–12

The National Standards for Music Education were developed by the Music Educators National Conference. Reprinted by permission.

Music

The study of music contributes in important ways to the quality of every student's life. Every musical work is a product of its time and place, although some works transcend their original settings and continue to appeal to humans through their timeless and universal attraction. Through singing, playing instruments and composing, students can express themselves creatively, while a knowledge of notation and performance traditions enables them to learn new music independently throughout their lives. Skills in analysis, evaluation and synthesis are important because they enable students to recognize and pursue excellence in the musical experiences and to understand and enrich their environment. Because music is an integral part of human history, the ability to listen with understanding is essential if students are to gain a broad cultural and historical perspective. The adult life of every student is enriched by the skills, knowledge and habits acquired in the study of music.

Every course in music, including performance courses, should provide instruction in creating, performing, listening to and analyzing music, in addition to focusing on its specific subject matter.

1. **Content Standard:** Singing, alone and with others, a varied repertoire of music
   Achievement Standard, Proficient:
   Students
   a. sing with *expression and *technical accuracy a large and varied repertoire of vocal literature with a *level of difficulty of 4, on a scale of 1 to 6, including some songs performed from memory
   b. sing music written in four parts, with and without accompaniment
   c. demonstrate well-developed ensemble skills
   Achievement Standard, Advanced:
   Students
   d. sing with expression and technical accuracy a large and varied repertoire of vocal literature with a level of difficulty of 5, on a scale of 1 to 6
   e. sing music written in more than four parts
   f. sing in small ensembles with one student on a part

2. **Content Standard:** Performing on instruments, alone and with others, a varied repertoire of music
   Achievement Standard, Proficient:
   Students
   a. perform with expression and technical accuracy a large and varied repertoire of instrumental literature with a level of difficulty of 4, on a scale of 1 to 6
   b. perform an appropriate part in an ensemble, demonstrating well-developed

ensemble skills
  c. perform in small ensembles with one student on a part

Achievement Standard, Advanced:
Students
  d. perform with expression and technical accuracy a large and varied repertoire of instrumental literature with a level of difficulty of 5, on a scale of 1 to 6.

3. **Content Standard:** Improvising melodies, variations and accompaniments
  Achievement Standard, Proficient:
Students
  a. improvise stylistically appropriate harmonizing parts
  b. improvise rhythmic and melodic variations on given pentatonic melodies and melodies in major and minor keys
  c. improvise original melodies over given chord progressions, each in a consistent *style, *meter and *tonality

  Achievement Standard, Advanced:
Students
  d. improvise stylistically appropriate harmonizing parts in a variety of styles
  e. improvise original melodies in a variety of styles, over given chord progressions, each in a consistent style, meter and tonality

4. **Content Standard:** Composing and arranging music within specified guidelines
  Achievement Standard, Proficient:
Students
  a. compose music in several distinct styles, demonstrating creativity in using the *elements of music for expressive effect
  b. arrange pieces for voices or instruments other than those for which the pieces were written in ways that preserve or enhance the expressive effect of the music
  c. compose and arrange music for voices and various acoustic and electronic instruments, demonstrating knowledge of the ranges and traditional usages of the sound sources

  Achievement Standard, Advanced:
Students
  d. compose music, demonstrating imagination and technical skill in applying the principles of composition

5. **Content Standard:** Reading and notating music
  Achievement Standard, Proficient:
Students
  a. demonstrate the ability to read an instrumental or vocal score of up to four *staves by describing how the elements of music are used
Students who participate in a choral or instrumental ensemble or class
  b. sight-read, accurately and expressively, music with a level of difficulty of 3, on a scale of 1 to 6

Achievement Standard, Advanced:

Students

    c. demonstrate the ability to read a full instrumental or vocal score by describing how the elements of music are used and explaining all transpositions and clefs

    d. interpret nonstandard notation symbols used by some 20th century [sic] composers

Students who participate in a choral or instrumental ensemble or class

    e. sight-read, accurately and expressively, music with a level of difficulty of 4, on a scale of 1 to 6

6. **Content Standard:** Listening to, analyzing and describing music

    Achievement Standard, Proficient:

Students

    a. analyze aural examples of a varied repertoire of music, representing diverse *genres and cultures, by describing the uses of elements of music and expressive devices

    b. demonstrate extensive knowledge of the technical vocabulary of music

    c. identify and explain compositional devices and techniques used to provide unity and variety and tension and release in a musical work and give examples of other works that make similar uses of these devices and techniques

Achievement Standard, Advanced:

Students

    d. demonstrate the ability to perceive and remember music events by describing in detail significant events[1] occurring in a given aural example

    e. compare ways in which musical materials are used in a given example relative to ways they are used in other works of the same genre or style

    f. analyze and describe uses of the elements of music in a given work that make it unique, interesting and expressive

7. **Content Standard:** Evaluating music and music performances

    Achievement Standard, Proficient:

Students

    a. evolve specific criteria for making informed, critical evaluations of the quality and effectiveness of performances, compositions, arrangements and improvisations and apply the criteria in their personal participation in music

    b. evaluate a performance, composition, arrangement or improvisation by comparing it to similar or exemplary models

    Achievement Standard, Advanced:

Students

    c. evaluate a given musical work in terms of its aesthetic qualities and explaining the musical means is uses to evoke feelings and emotions

8. **Content Standard:** Understanding relationships between music, the other arts, and disciplines outside the arts

Achievement Standard, Proficient:

Students

    a. explain how elements, artistic processes (such as imagination or craftsmanship), and organizational principles (such as unity and variety or repetition and contrast) are used in similar and distinctive ways in the various arts and cite examples

    b. compare characteristics of two or more arts within a particular historical period or style and cite examples from various cultures

    c. explain ways in which the principles and subject matter of various disciplines outside the arts are interrelated with those of music[2]

Achievement Standard, Advanced:

Students

    d. compare the uses of characteristic elements, artistic processes and organizational principles among the arts in different historical periods and different cultures

    e. explain how the roles of creators, performers, and others involved in the production and presentation of the arts are similar to and different from one another in the various arts[3]

9. **Content Standard:** Understanding music in relation to history and culture

Achievement Standard, Proficient:

Students

    a. classify by genre or style and by historical period or culture unfamiliar but representative aural examples of music and explain the reasoning behind their classifications

    b. identify sources of American music genres,[4] trace the evolution of those genres, and cite well-known musicians associated with them

    c. identify various roles[5] that musicians perform, cite representative individuals who have functioned in each role, and describe their activities and achievements

Achievement Standard, Advanced:

Students

    d. identify and explain the stylistic features of a given musical work that serve to define its aesthetic tradition and its historical or cultural context

    e. identify and describe music genres or styles that show the influence of two or more cultural traditions, identify the cultural source of each influence, and trace the historical conditions that produced the synthesis of influences

Terms identified by an asterisk (*) are explained further in the glossary of National Standards for Arts Education, published by Music Educators National Conference, © 1994.

1. E.g., fugal entrances, chromatic modulations, developmental devices
2. E.g., language arts: compare the ability of music and literature to convey images, feeling and meanings; physics: describe the physical basis of tone production in string, wind, percussion and electronic instruments and the human voice and of the transmission and perception of sound
3. E.g., creators: painters, composers, choreographers, playwrights; performers: instrumentalists, singers, dancers, actors; others: conductors, costumers, directors, lighting designers
4. E.g., swing, Broadway musical, blues
5. E.g., entertainer, teacher, transmitter of cultural tradition

CHAPTER OVERVIEWS • FOCUSES • EVALUATION ANSWERS

Book Overview

Throughout this skill bank book, advanced concepts in pitch and rhythm, along with music terminology definitions, are presented. Exercises to practice are included for each concept. The Evaluation pages at the end of each chapter assess the concepts presented in each chapter.

Chapter One Overview

In Chapter One, the Circle of Fifths is presented. Formation of key signatures by adding sharps and flats is explained. Additional pitch concepts of major, minor and chromatic scales are introduced. Tonic, subdominant and dominant diatonic chords are defined. Practice exercises are provided for all 12 major and minor scales, along with their diatonic chords. Modes and modal scales are introduced.

Chapter One Focus

- Sight-read, accurately and expressively, music with a level of difficulty of 5, on a scale of 1 to 6. *(NS 5e)*
- Demonstrate extensive knowledge of the technical vocabulary of music. *(NS 6b)*

Chapter One Evaluation

Answers to Questions on page 11:
- *First Bullet: The Circle of Fifths*
  Clockwise, starting at C major/A minor, G major/E minor, D major/B minor, A major/F♯ minor, E major/C♯ minor, B major or C♭ major/G♯ minor or A♭ minor, F♯ major or G♭ major/D♯ minor or E♭ minor, C♯ major or D♭ major/A♯ minor or B♭ minor, A♭ major/F minor, E♭ major/C minor, B♭ major/G minor, F major/D minor.

- *Second Bullet: Sight-Singing Exercise*
  Check for accurate pitch and rhythm while maintaining a steady beat. The Dorian mode is used in this exercise.

Chapter Two Overview

In Chapter Two, the rhythmic concepts of note and rest relationships are presented. Time signatures, meter and conducting patterns are given for common simple meter and compound meter examples. Asymmetrical meters are introduced, along with sample conducting patterns. Triplet and duplet concepts are explained, and examples of each are provided in all note values. Practice exercises are provided for each concept.

Chapter Two Focus

- Compose music, demonstrating imagination and technical skill in applying the principles of composition. *(NS 4d)*
- Sight-read, accurately and expressively, music with a level of difficulty of 5, on a scale of 1 to 6. *(NS 5e)*
- Demonstrate extensive knowledge of the technical vocabulary of music. *(NS 6b)*

Chapter Two Evaluation

Answers to Questions on page 22:
- *First Bullet: Be A Composer*
  Each rhythm pattern will be different. Check for accurate note and rest combinations within the requested time signature. Give students the opportunity to clap or play their patterns.

Chapter Three Overview

In Chapter Three, diatonic intervals are

introduced. Solfège syllables and numbers are given for each interval. Major, minor, augmented and diminished intervals are defined. Practice exercises for each interval are provided.

Chapter Three Focus

• Sight-read, accurately and expressively, music with a level of difficulty of 5, on a scale of 1 to 6. *(NS 5e)*
• Demonstrate extensive knowledge of the technical vocabulary of music. *(NS 6b)*

Chapter Three Evaluation

Answers to Questions on page 43:

• *First Bullet: True or False?*
  (1) False; an interval is the relationship of one pitch to another; **(2)** True.
• *Second Bullet: Identify the Intervals*
  (1) Major sixth; **(2)** Major third; **(3)** Perfect fourth; **(4)** Major seventh; **(5)** Major second; **(6)** Perfect fifth.
• *Third Bullet: Sight-Singing Melodies*
  (1) Major sixth; **(2)** Augmented fourth; **(3)** Minor third; **(4)** Perfect fourth; **(5)** Prime; **(6)** Perfect fifth; **(7)** Major second; **(8)** Minor second; **(9)** Minor seventh; **(10)** Major third. Check for accurate pitch and rhythm patterns while maintaining a steady beat.

Chapter Four Overview

In Chapter Four, concepts of simple and compound meter are further explained. Division of the beat is presented. Conducting diagrams are given for two, three and four-beat patterns. Ties, dotted rhythms, "short-long" patterns and rests are also described. Practice exercises are included for each concept.

Chapter Four Focus

• Compose music, demonstrating imagination and technical skill in applying the principles of composition. *(NS 4d)*
• Sight-read, accurately and expressively,

music with a level difficulty of 5, on a scale of 1 to 6. *(NS 5d)*
• Demonstrate extensive knowledge of the technical vocabulary of music. *(NS 6b)*

Chapter Four Evaluation

Answers to Questions on page 59:

• *First Bullet: Meter Identification*
  (1) simple; **(2)** compound; **(3)** simple; **(4)** simple; **(5)** compound; **(6)** simple; **(7)** simple; **(8)** compound; **(9)** simple.
• *Second Bullet: Musical Math*
  (1) True; **(2)** False; need quarter note or quarter rest on right side of equation; **(3)** False; need a quarter note or quarter rest on right side of equation; **(4)** False; quarter note needs a dot on right side of equation; **(5)** True; **(6)** False; need to remove a dotted quarter note from the right side of the equation.
• *Third Bullet: Be A Composer*
  Each composition will be different. Check for accurate rhythm while maintaining a steady beat.
• *Fourth Bullet: Challenge*
  Check for accurate pitch and rhythm during performance. Discuss lyric choices.

Chapter Five Overview

In Chapter Five, chromatic alteration in melodies is introduced. Definitions of sharps, flats and naturals are presented. Solfège syllables are given for each chromatic alteration. Practice exercises are given for each altered pitch.

Chapter Five Focus

• Sight-read, accurately and expressively, music with a level of difficulty of 5, on a scale of 1 to 6. *(NS 5e)*
• Demonstrate extensive knowledge of the technical vocabulary of music. *(NS 6b)*

Chapter Five Evaluation

Answers to Questions on page 70:

- *First Bullet: Review Chromatic Scales*
  Check for accurate pitch and syllables/note names.
- *Second Bullet: Sight-Singing Exercises*
  Check for accurate pitch and rhythm. Exercise 1 is in F major. Exercise 2 is in G major. Exercise 3 is in D major.

Chapter Six Overview

In Chapter Six, concepts of simple and compound meter are further developed. Subdivision of the beat is introduced. Less common meters are presented. Concepts of cut time, tied notes, dotted rhythms, "short-long" patterns and rests are developed. Practice exercises are given for each concept.

Chapter Six Focus

- Sight-read, accurately and expressively, music with a level of difficulty of 5, on a scale of 1 to 6. *(NS 5b)*
- Demonstrate extensive knowledge of the technical vocabulary of music. *(NS 6b)*

Chapter Six Evaluation

Answers to Questions on page 86:

- *First Bullet: Mystery Meters*
  (1) 2/2 (cut time) or 4/4 and simple; **(2)** 3/8 and simple; **(3)** 9/8 and compound; **(4)** 3/2 and simple or 6/4 and compound; **(5)** 6/8 and compound; **(6)** 2/2 (cut time) or 4/4 and simple; **(7)** 2/4 or 4/8 and simple; **(8)** 3/4 and simple. Check for accurate rhythm while maintaining a steady beat.

Chapter Seven Overview

In Chapter Seven, non-diatonic intervals are introduced. Practice exercises with non-diatonic intervals are provided in many major and minor keys.

Chapter Seven Focus

- Sight-read, accurately and expressively, music with a level of difficulty of 5, on a scale of 1 to 6. *(NS 5b)*
- Demonstrate extensive knowledge of the technical vocabulary of music. *(NS 6b)*

Chapter Seven Evaluation

Answers to Questions on page 108:

- *First Bullet: Vocabulary*
  (1) Octave; **(2)** Non-Diatonic Major Third; **(3)** Non-Diatonic Diminished Fifth; **(4)** Prime; **(5)** Non-Diatonic Interval
- *Second Bullet: Identify the Non-Diatonic Intervals*
  (1) minor third; **(2)** minor third; **(3)** octave.
- *Third Bullet: Challenge*
  Check for accurate rhythms and correct conducting patterns.

Chapter Eight Overview

In Chapter Eight, the rhythmic concept of mixed meter is presented. Examples of directions in beat or the division of the beat during meter change are given. Asymmetrical meters are further defined. Triplet and duplet rhythmic concepts are further defined. Practice exercises are given for each concept.

Chapter Eight Focus

- Compose music, demonstrating imagination and technical skill in applying the principles of composition. *(NS 4d)*
- Sight-read, accurately and expressively, music with a level of difficulty of 5, on a scale of 1 to 6. *(NS 5e)*
- Demonstrate extensive knowledge of the technical vocabulary of music. *(NS 6b)*

Chapter Eight Evaluation

Answers to Questions on page 117:

- *First Bullet: Be A Conductor*
  Check for accurate placement of beat numbers within the conducting patterns.

- *Second Bullet: Be A Composer*
Each composition will be different. Check for correct rhythms. Provide students the opportunity to play their compositions on rhythm instruments.
- *Third Bullet: Challenge*
Additional opportunity to add pitches and transfer to a staff will require a review for accuracy of key choice, chromatic alteration, notes and rhythm patterns.

Chapter Nine Overview

In Chapter Nine, the pitch concept of modulation is defined. Examples of various kinds of modulation including relative major/minor keys, common chord, common tone, chromatic and enharmonic are included. Practice exercises in each form of modulation are presented.

Chapter Nine Focus

- Sing music written in four parts, with and without accompaniment. (*NS 1b*)
- Demonstrate the ability to read a vocal score of up to four staves by describing how the elements of music are used. (*NS 5a*)
- Sight-read, accurately and expressively, music with a level of difficulty of 5, on a scale of 1 to 6. (*NS 5e*)
- Demonstrate extensive knowledge of the technical vocabulary of music. (*NS 6b*)

Chapter Nine Evaluation

Answers to Questions on page 128:
- *First Bullet: Modulation Methods*
(**1**) Chromatic; (**2**) Enharmonic; (**3**) Common Chord
- *Second Bullet: Modulation Methods*
The pivot chord in Exercise 3 is the first chord in measure 2.

Chapter Ten Overview

In Chapter Ten, the pitch concepts of polytonal and atonal melodies are defined. Fixed *do* is used. Practice exercises in various keys are provided to reinforce atonal music.

Chapter Ten Focus

- Demonstrate the ability to read a vocal score of up to four staves by describing how the elements of music are used. (*NS 5a*)
- Sight-read, accurately and expressively, music with a level of difficulty of 5, on a scale of 1 to 6. (*NS 5e*)
- Demonstrate extensive knowledge of the technical vocabulary of music. (*NS 6b*)

Chapter Ten Evaluation

Answers to Questions on page 134:
- *First Bullet: Fixed* Do *Challenge*
(**1**) *sol* to *re*; (**2**) *ra* to *ma*; (**3**) *mi* to *le*; (**4**) *do* to *re*; (**5**) *ti* to *le*; (**6**) *fi* to *sol*; (**7**) *re* to *ma*; (**8**) *do* to *do*; (**9**) *ti* to *te*; (**10**) *la* to *re*. Check for accurate pitches.
- *Second Bullet: Be A Composer*
Each composition will be different. Check for correct rhythm and fixed *do* syllables. Provide students the opportunity to sing or play their compositions.

Pitch

◆ **Sight-Singing Method • Movable *Do* in Major Keys**
Regardless of the key, *do* is always the first pitch of the scale.

◆ **Diatonic Scales**

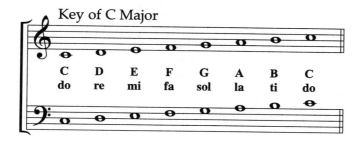

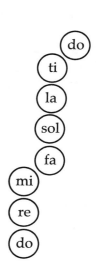

◆ **Chromatic Scales**

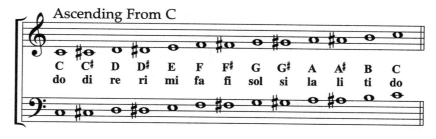

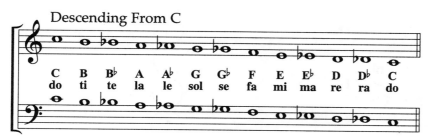

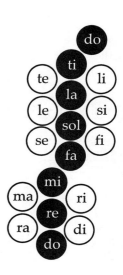

Pitch

◆ **Sight-Singing Method • Movable *Do* in Minor Keys**
Regardless of the key, *la* is always the first pitch of the scale.

◆ **The Natural Minor Scale**

Key of A Minor

A	B	C	D	E	F	G	A
la	ti	do	re	mi	fa	sol	la

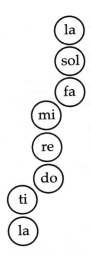

◆ **The Harmonic Minor Scale**

Key of D Minor

D	E	F	G	A	B♭	C♯	D
la	ti	do	re	mi	fa	si	la

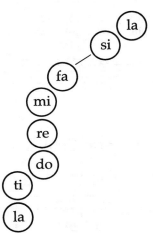

◆ **The Melodic Minor Scale**

Key of E Minor

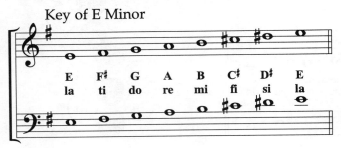

E	F♯	G	A	B	C♯	D♯	E
la	ti	do	re	mi	fi	si	la

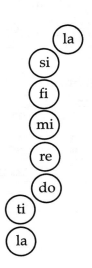

Pitch

◆ **Sight-Singing Method • Fixed *Do* in Major Keys**

Regardless of the key, *do* is always C.

◆ **Diatonic Scales**

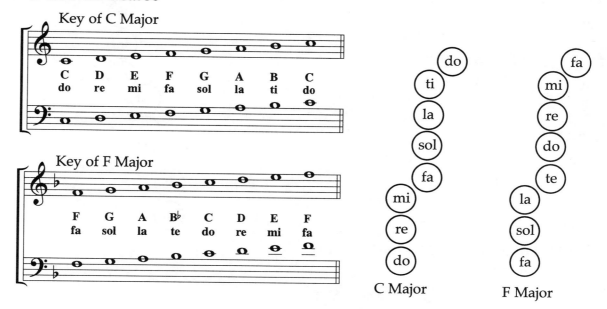

C Major   F Major

◆ **Chromatic Scales**

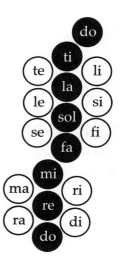

Pitch

◆ **Sight-Singing Method • Fixed *Do* in Minor Keys**

Regardless of the key, *la* is always A.

◆ **The Natural Minor Scale**

Key of A Minor

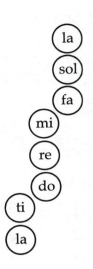

◆ **The Harmonic Minor Scale**

Key of D Minor

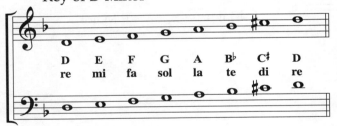

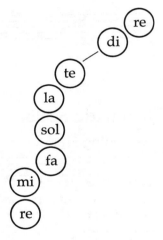

◆ **The Melodic Minor Scale**

Key of E Minor

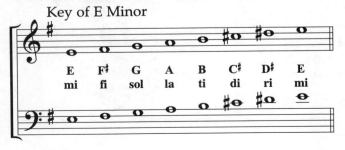

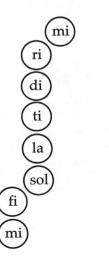

Pitch

◆ **Sight-Singing Method • Numbers in Major Keys**
Regardless of the key, "1" is always the first pitch of the scale.

◆ **Diatonic Scales**

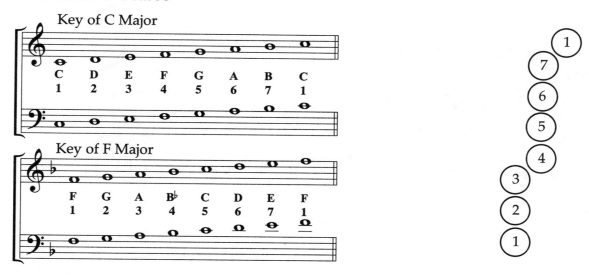

Accidentals can be performed either by singing the number but raising or lowering the pitch by a half step, or by singing the word "sharp" or "flat" before the number as a grace note.

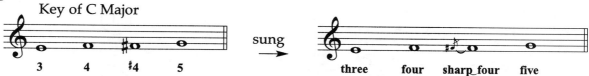

◆ **Chromatic Scales**

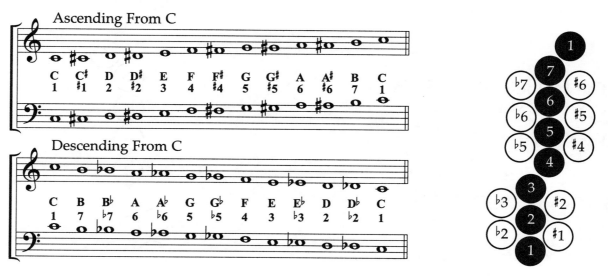

Pitch

◆ **Sight-Singing Method • Numbers in Minor Keys**
Regardless of the key, "6" is always the first pitch of the scale.

◆ **The Natural Minor Scale**

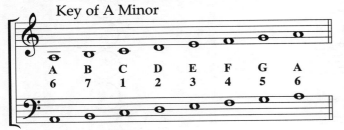

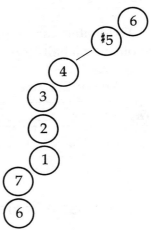

◆ **The Harmonic Minor Scale**

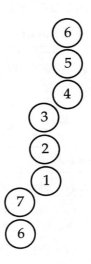

◆ **The Melodic Minor Scale**

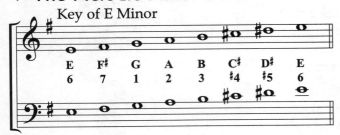

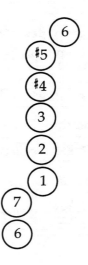

Rhythm

◆ Counting Methods • Simple Meter

Following are three methods in use for counting rhythms in simple meter.

Kodály	Traditional	Eastman

Rhythm

◆ Counting Methods • Simple Meter

Kodály

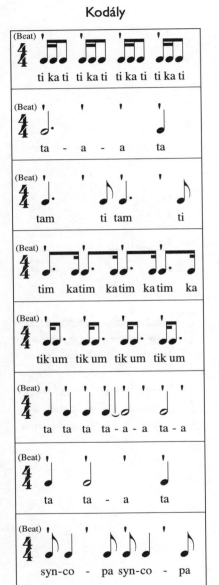

Traditional

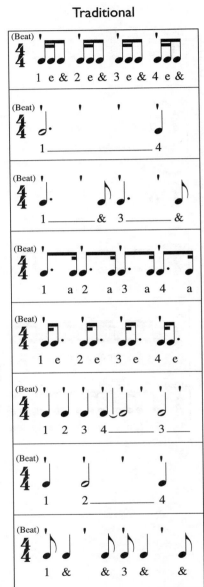

Eastman

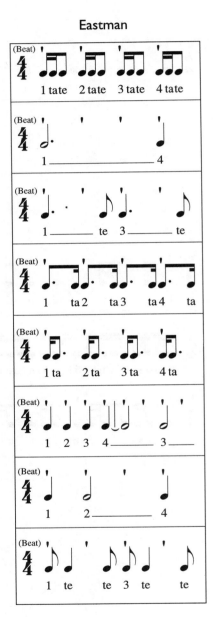

Rhythm

◆ Counting Methods • Compound Meter

Following are three methods in use for counting rhythms in compound meter.

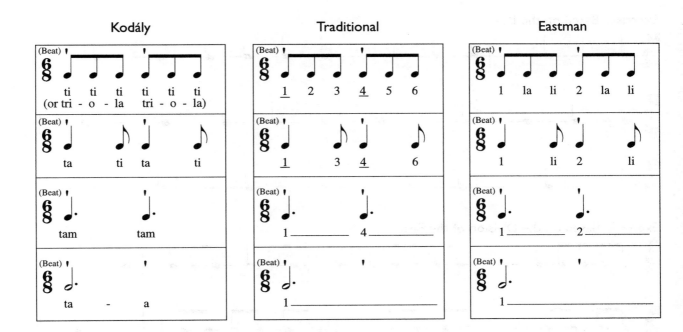

Practice

◆ Rhythm • Simple Meter
Clap, tap, or chant while conducting the following exercises.

Exercises Based on the Beat

Exercises Based on the Division of the Beat

Exercises Based on the Subdivision of the Beat

Practice

◆ Rhythm • Dotted Notes

Clap, tap, or chant while conducting the following exercises.

Exercises with Dotted Half Notes

Exercises with Dotted Quarter Notes

Exercises with Dotted Eighth Notes

Practice

◆ Rhythm • **Compound Meter**
Clap, tap, or chant while conducting the following exercises.

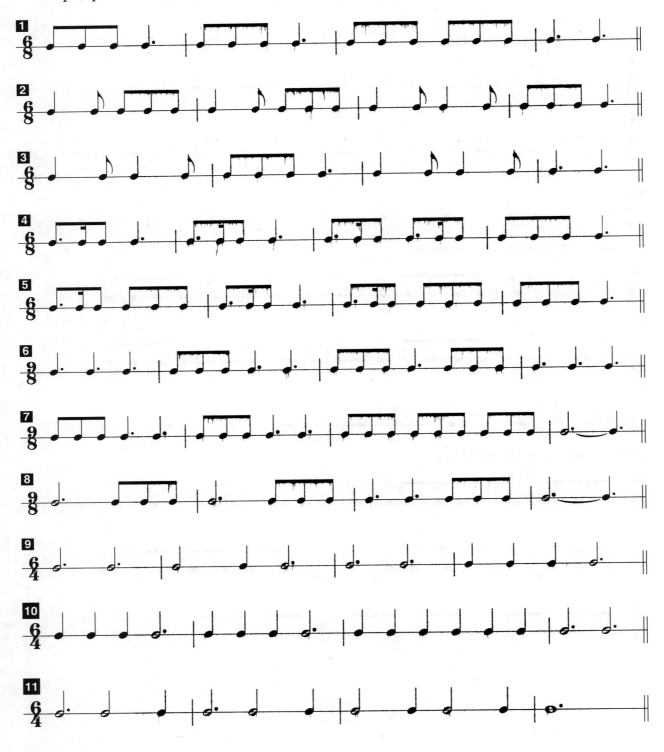

Pitch

◆ The Circle of Fifths

In music, the relationship between each key is based on a perfect fifth. A **perfect fifth** is *an interval of two pitches that are five notes apart on the staff.* An easy way to visualize this relationship is on the keyboard.

Study the keyboard below. Notice that if you start on C and move to the left by the distance of a fifth, you will find the keys that contain flats. Notice that the number of flats in each key signature increases by one each time you move one perfect fifth to the left.

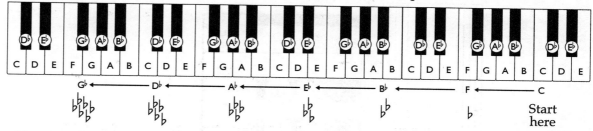

However, if you start on C and move to the right by the distance of a fifth, you will find the keys that contain sharps. Notice that the number of sharps in each key signature increases by one each time you move one perfect fifth to the right.

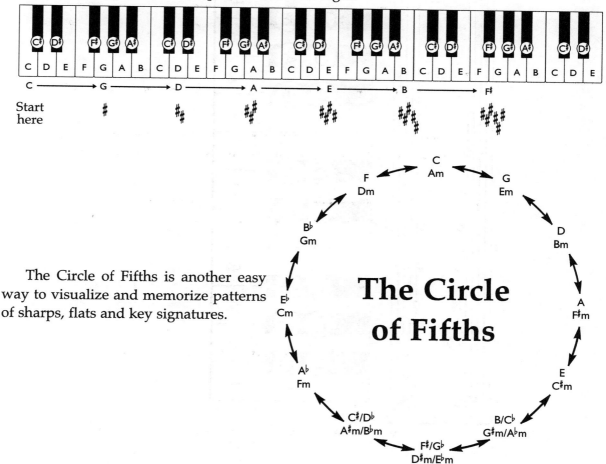

The Circle of Fifths is another easy way to visualize and memorize patterns of sharps, flats and key signatures.

Pitch

◆ **The Piano Keyboard**

For use with Sight-Singing exercises. Use the keyboard and **notation on this page to** identify and perform the notes in your voice part.

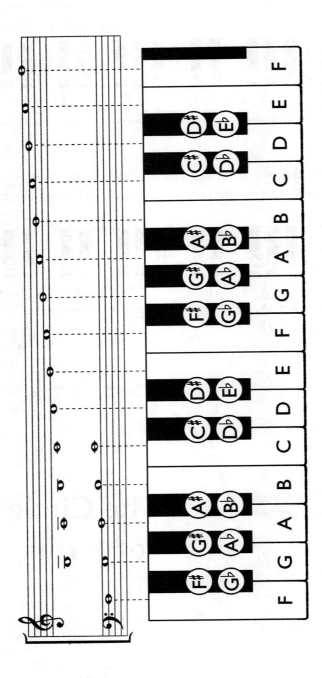